Your Ideal
Hawaii
Home

Avoid Disaster when Buying or Building in Hawaii

Tyler Mercier
Chris Mercier

ISBN: **1467921114**
ISBN-13: **978-1467921114**

Library of Congress Control Number: **2011-960799**

Photos, art, layout, and design by authors.

ACKNOWLEGEMENTS

We could not have written this book without the stories and advice from the hundreds of people we have met in Hawaii. We appreciate the time people in Hawaii have taken to answer our endless questions. We are grateful to everyone who read our hiloliving blogs and website on the topics in this book. We have learned so much from the questions and comments our readers have sent to us and the meetings and email exchanges we have had with people considering a move to Hawaii. We thank our friends in Hilo for their years of inspiration, particularly the wonderful water aerobics group at the NAS pool. We are very grateful to Lois and Bill Hodges for taking the time to proofread our draft and offer us helpful comments. We thank our friends in Alii Cove for their stories about successful real estate purchases in Hawaii. We want to acknowledge our son Daniel for his endless patience, advice, and support during the two years we have been writing this book.

CONTENTS

Introduction

At the first homeowners association meeting we attended on Hawaii Island, a new retiree, who had just completed construction of her dream home in Hawaii, pulled out a wad of tissues and started sobbing, "if only I had known, I would have never built this house here…. If only I had known…". Since that meeting over eight years ago, we have met hundreds of newcomers to Hawaii that regret the house design they built or the location they selected and have grumbled to us, "if only I had known…". This book was inspired from years of hearing stories by people who bought houses, condos, lots, or built a house in Hawaii only to discover that what they did not know about Hawaii's climate, culture, laws, and communities turned their dream home into a nightmare. They discovered the hard way that a perfect house or great location on the mainland US and Canada or in Europe can be a disaster on a remote, tropical island in Hawaii.

The climate in Hawaii confuses newcomers because there are dramatic variations within small areas on each island. These unique microclimates are created by the changes in altitude from sea level to the summits of the volcanoes and the effects of the moisture-filled trade winds. Newcomers often assume that all of Hawaii has the same weather as the hotels in Waikiki or the other coastal resort areas of Hawaii. Instead of the sun-drenched tropical paradise they expected, they find themselves with a home in a perpetual rain cloud with over 200 inches of rain a year. New property owners have been shocked to discover that state laws allow farming operations inside some gated residential communities and that Hawaiians may have a legal right to come on their property to grow food or have a religious ceremony. Being knowledgeable about Hawaii's unique climate, property laws, and culture increases your probability of finding a home and community that is the right fit for you and your family's lifestyle.

The topics covered in this book are focused on the questions people have asked us in person and emails after reading our blogs and websites about living in Hawaii. We are not realtors, architects, builders or lawyers. We share the information as a friend living in Hawaii would, rather than from the perspective of a realtor or a guide book.

We have had the benefit of living in the tropics in high school, where we met on the island of Java. Though we have lived in wonderful towns and cities across the US and visited incredible places in Europe and Asia, our dream has always been to live in Hawaii. We started visiting the islands every year in the late 1990s, and in 2007 we moved to the island of Hawaii. We lived two years in Hilo town near the University of Hawaii in a post and pier house and two years on the Kona coast where we currently live in condominium complex. Though many of our experiences are based on Hawaii Island, we believe that the topics covered in this book are important to know before building or buying a home anywhere in the state.

We think that Hawaii is the most wonderful place in the world and a paradise for people prepared for the tropics and willing to accommodate the unique aspects of the islands.

This book gives an overview of topics you should know about Hawaii before building or buying a home. It is filled with diagrams and photographs to help describe house design features and climate zone differences to allow you to quickly grasp the points. References are provided for further research on any of the topics. We hope that this book allows you to find your ideal home in Hawaii and avoid the disaster that others have had by "not knowing".

Chapter One
A Hawaii Style House

The Wrong House in Hawaii

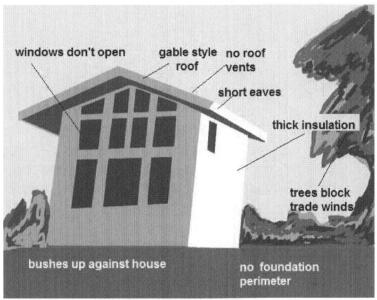

cold-climate house diagram

The perfect style house for Seattle, Cape Cod, or other cold climates can become an overheated, mold-growing, bug-infested, nightmare house when built in Hawaii. Many people who are new to Hawaii and a tropical climate build their Hawaiian dream house using a design and building materials for the climate they just came from on the mainland. This mistake means they run their air conditioning around the clock to keep comfortable and have extra maintenance to keep their house intact in Hawaii's climate. Hours before the hottest part of the day, when our house is still cool from the tropical breezes, we hear the roar of air conditioners across the street struggling to pump heat out of cold-climate style houses. The short eaves of these houses let the sunlight stream in the windows from early morning and thick insulation in the walls holds the heat in, creating a solar oven. Depending on air conditioning to keep a house cool and dry is very expensive in Hawaii since electricity costs 5 to 10 times more than on the mainland.

A house designed to deal with heat, rain, humidity, and bugs is ideal in Hawaii. During the rainy season, water pours down for long periods filling drainage ditches to the brim and turning streets into rivers. Houses built with garages and gardens set below street level can completely fill with water during the rainy season. Standing water creates the perfect environment for mosquitoes, mold, and mildew. In addition, any wood touching the wet ground or concrete will rot.

Though they appear pleasing to the eye of someone use to the architecture, cold-climate style houses are not fun to live in. Most people move to Hawaii for its delightful tropical climate, but living in these types of houses will actually force you to breathe conditioned air and shut the weather out. A short, steep roof helps deal with heavy snowfall and collects heat, but that design in Hawaii's climate creates a solar collector that overheats the top of the house and can only be alleviated by an attic fan or at least windows that open or vents that allow airflow. Multiple stories can create cozy, warm rooms upstairs in a cold climate, but in Hawaii it makes living upstairs miserable without a way to mitigate the heat on each level.

Before buying or building a house in Hawaii, make sure you are not recreating cold-climate architecture in the tropics. Familiar house designs for the mainland may make living in a cold environment more bearable and even minimize utilities, but in Hawaii, this type of house will have the opposite effect of being miserably hot during the day and costly to cool and upkeep. Worse, it separates you from Hawaii's cooling breezes and tropical climate.

A House Designed for Hawaii

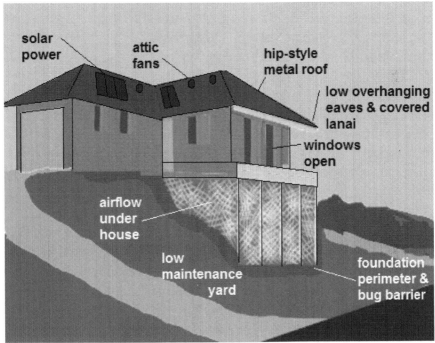

Hawaii-style house diagram

Living in a house designed for Hawaii's tropical climate and with the right features is substantially more enjoyable, healthy, and costs far less than other designs. The best Hawaii designs reduce dampness, pests, keep the house cool, and lower the electric bill. These designs have low pitch roofs with long over-hanging eaves that keep the rain out, block the sun from inside the house, and cover the lanai (Hawaii

7

porch). Hawaii's air is warm and humid so keeping the house dry with airflow avoids an endless battle with mold and mildew. Many of the best house features for Hawaii that would be drafty and miserable in a cold climate make life in Hawaii ideal.

The trade winds blow about 90% of the time in Hawaii. Locating a house so that it gets unobstructed access to these winds keeps it cooler and dryer. Airflow through the house means that air conditioning is not needed. Houses are often raised up on poles or geographically situated so that they are not blocked from the trade winds by hills, trees, or other structures. Windows are located in the house so that wind can blow end to end through the house, preferably in all directions. Windows must be able to open fully and have secure screens and security latches so that they can be left open all day and night to let the breezes cool the house.

Hawaii has the unusual factor of tropical trees that can grow ten feet or more every year. At that rate, they are as high as a five story building in five years. This growth can quickly destroy a view and block the critical airflow turning a cool, breezy house into a hot, humid house. Part of an ideal Hawaii house design is to make sure there is protected access to the trade winds.

Hawaii houses with low pitch, metal roofs, long overhanging eaves, and post and pier construction may look odd to people moving from a cold climate. However, a house elevated above the ground, with good airflow, and eaves that block direct sunlight allows you to enjoy the fabulous Hawaii weather and makes a big difference in lowering the total cost of living.

Post and Pier Design

Post and pier design house

Post and pier houses are very popular in Hawaii because they offer so many advantages in the tropical climate. They are the ideal design for cooling, bug control, and are cheaper to build than concrete foundations.

A post and pier house is elevated above the damp ground, crawling bugs, and any water from downpours or floods. The elevation of the structure above the ground allows airflow underneath the house, which keeps the house cooler and drier. Post and pier houses can be built in steep locations that would be challenging to pour a concrete slab foundation. The higher elevation can improve the view and better situate the house to get the tropical breezes.

Post and pier construction tends to be less expensive than concrete foundation houses. Concrete has to be shipped to Hawaii from the mainland and the expertise to install heavy rebar in the foundation to protect against earthquake damage is not common. Digging trenches for pipes in lava is expensive and time consuming and a cracked or damaged concrete slab foundation is harder to repair. In contrast, post and pier construction requires only concrete footings and the water and sewer pipes fit in the space under the house.

Most post and pier houses use borate salt treated wood for the posts, one of the few approved methods of protecting wood from termites in Hawaii. For centuries, builders in Hawaii have used salt to protect wood from bugs and mold. They threw logs into the ocean and then dried them out once the wood was encrusted with salt. However, the benefit of borate treated wood is lost if lanais or wood stairs attached to the house are built from untreated plywood. Termites will quickly enter a house to munch on untreated wood and cabinets. Wooden posts also need protection from standing water. Though it is standard practice to secure wood posts with footings or metal post bases, we commonly see wood posts supporting staircases of newly built houses and condominiums in Hawaii rotting in standing water.

Though the advantages seem to make post and pier houses ideal, they have some significant drawbacks for some people. Not everyone wants to climb a staircase to get into the house. The lanais are higher above the ground and it is not easy to childproof railings. They also tend to amplify the feeling of earthquakes so that even small earthquakes can cause a post and pier house to sway back and forth. Some experts claim that post and pier houses will not be as safe as houses with slab concrete foundations in a major earthquake. They recommend extra bracing under the house for post and pier houses to protect against earthquakes. Moreover, they are more susceptible to damage from high winds and in urban areas the noise can be an issue and privacy reduced due to the elevation above the road.

A Hawaii Hip–style Roof

Hawaii metal hip-style roof

Structural engineers recommend hip-style roofs with long overhanging eaves as the best design for dealing with high winds, hurricanes, and earthquakes. Hip-style roofs are aerodynamically superior to other roof types because they have bracing as a part of their design. Gable style roofs, popular on the mainland, do poorly in Hawaii's high winds and earthquakes and require extra bracing to keep the gable end from collapsing in high winds.

long overhanging eaves

In Hawaii, long overhanging eaves block the sun from shining directly into the windows and onto the walls of the house keeping the house significantly cooler. The length of overhang should be about five feet or more. During heavy rain, the overhang allows the windows and doors to remain open without getting the interior wet. Open windows and doors keep the air blowing through the house, the rooms cool, the air fresh, and the bugs away.

Houses with multiple stories are best with overhanging eaves at each level to provide protection from the sun for every story. The eaves should also extend the length of the lanai around the house. Direct sun on to the lanai can cause sun damage to anyone sitting there as well as the building materials themselves. Rain and sun will quickly disintegrate uncovered wood lanais and stairs in Hawaii.

Metal roofs are a popular choice for Hawaii houses. They reflect the heat, readily deal with rain, are bug proof, fire proof, and can handle the rapid changes in temperature during the day. Though they rust, they can be reconditioned or replaced in sections. On the wet sides of the Hawaiian Islands, metal and tile roofs are the only way to keep from having a mold-saturated roof. Surprisingly, many houses in Hawaii have shingle or shake roofs, which quickly turn green and then black with mold in the rain and humidity.

The roof must support the weight and proper positioning of solar panels. Solar power makes sense to minimize the use of electricity in Hawaii. Solar water heaters are required by law for any new homes being built in Hawaii and they are a good idea to add to any house that does not already have a system installed. We had an electric water heater in our rental house which we had to keep turned off most of the time to conserve electricity. Numerous programs exist in Hawaii to help with the cost of installing solar power and the savings on electric bills is substantial.

Foundation Perimeter and Bug Barriers

foundation perimeter around house

Unlike cold climates where the insects die in the winter, bugs and insects thrive in the soil all year long in Hawaii. A foundation perimeter around the house is a way to create a barrier for bugs, foliage, and water runoff.

13

The typical foundation perimeter consists of gravel or lava stones about 18 to 24 inches wide around the house. The gravel is contained by large rail ties or treated wood on either side. The foundation perimeter keeps vegetation from growing up against the house, which allows unobstructed airflow around and under the house and discourages bugs looking for dark, moist hideouts. Keeping the perimeter weeded or sprayed with herbicide regularly clearly separates the yard from the house foundation and makes any water damage or bug invasions easy to spot.

concrete footing for post and pier house with metal flange

A post and pier house needs a metal bug barrier between every concrete footing and wooden post to keep the bugs from crawling up the post to enter the house. The metal bug barriers are thin pieces of metal that overhang the concrete footing and bend downward making it nearly impossible for bugs to get around them to crawl up the post. Many new houses in Hawaii are missing this important bug protection or have the metal pieces installed upside down. If you add a little pesticide to the underside of this barrier, it makes it almost impossible for most bugs to get past.

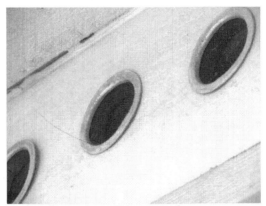

roof vents with metal screens

Bugs, birds, and rodents can get into a house through roof vents. In most places vents are covered with heavy screen material or metal screens. In Hawaii, however, that type of vent cover will quickly dissolve in the salty sea air and bugs and birds will rapidly move in. Effective vent covers in Hawaii are chrome plated steel with heavy-duty fine screen behind. The best approach is to have vents located so that you can see if they are intact and easily replace them. Any unscreened, open spaces can be a problem and even a tiny crack where a screen is bent can be a way into the house for the uninvited bugs, geckos and rodents.

In Hawaii, a house designed with a foundation perimeter and protection against dampness and unwanted tropical pests is an ideal home.

Chapter Two
A Hawaii Designed Garden

Joy and Labor of a Hawaii Garden

tropical yard with fruit trees

We were never able to grow anything before moving to Hawaii and on the mainland any plant we bought usually died. In Hawaii it is the opposite for us, any plant we buy grows huge. We have bought chocolate trees, tea plants, coffee plants, and anything that caught our fancy at farmer's markets and they all flourished. The incredible tropical flowers and variety of fruit trees make gardens a special joy in Hawaii.

We were delighted with the lush green lawn and fruit trees behind our house when we moved to Hawaii. It was exciting to harvest bananas and coffee and we were amazed to watch how fast everything grew. The lawn seemed to grow an inch a day and even though we picked lemons almost every day, the tree was always overloaded with them.

overgrown foliage house

At first, the endless summer growth of Hawaii was a dream come true, however, after two years of constant mowing, trimming, and weeding, we started to see the appeal of the houses with a lava field for yards in our neighborhood. No matter how many times a week we worked in the yard, the lawn always needed to be mowed, the trees always needed to be trimmed, and lemons always needed to be picked before they rotted. We were unable to find an affordable gardener so our tropical garden began to feel like yard slavery. It was a revelation for us to experience the extent to which a Hawaiian garden required our time, effort, expense, and the level of exhaustion we had from the labor.

The climate in Hawaii extends the growing season to the entire year so there is never a time when there is a slowdown in growth and you get to rest from yard work. The constant growth creates a massive amount of green waste to be mulched or hauled off to the

17

dump. Working in a garden in Hawaii's hot, humid climate is more exhausting than working in cooler, temperate climates. Unlike the mainland, where you can get many bids to mow your lawn or trim the trees, labor is expensive and hard to find in Hawaii. We have watched houses disappear behind a wall of weeds ten feet tall within a few months after the residents stopped doing their yard work. Whenever we could not keep up with our yard, loud coqui frogs, mosquitoes, cockroaches, and foot long centipedes quickly moved in. We know a person that got lost on their one acre property because the fast growth of foliage blocked their view and made it impossible for them to see the landmarks they used to find their way back to their house.

Some people get out of the labor required to maintain a garden in Hawaii by living in a housing complex or condominium where maintenance of the grounds is managed by a homeowners association. The cost does not go away, since it is included as part of the owners association fee, however, it does free up the time and energy spent on yard work. Having the grounds maintenance handled by someone else does not mean all the discomfort of a tropical Hawaii yard goes away.

Hawaii shared condominium grounds

The noise of gardening crews using loud mowers and blowers for hours every day is a common complaint of residents along with the type and frequency of pesticide and herbicide use.

Many people consider their garden one of the joys of their Hawaii lifestyle, yet we know many others that regret the huge yards they purchased with their Hawaiian home because of the amount of labor it takes them to manage. If you decide to leave the growing to others, you will not miss out on the bounty of Hawaii thanks to farmer's markets around the islands and Hawaii's grocery stores carrying local grown fruits and vegetables.

Fast Plant Growth in Hawaii

Albizia tree growth blocking the sun in Puna

Trees and bushes grow quickly in Hawaii and can become a problem as their height soars. Monkeypod trees, for example, can grow up to 80 feet with a 100-foot diameter canopy. During two years living in Hilo, large portions of our view disappeared as our

19

neighbor's palm trees grew up. We have met homeowners that not only lost the ocean view from their porch but also lost their cooling ocean breezes from the growth of trees.

We were surprised to find out that banana trees can grow over 25 feet tall. Cutting down a heavy bunch of bananas hanging over twenty feet above our heads was a new experience for us. Our first attempt, before we learned how to carefully cut the tree down to harvest, resulted in a collapsed ladder and 60 pounds of bananas landing on top of us as we crumpled to the ground. Banana trees produce just once and then die, requiring that the huge, sticky, juicy, trunk be cut down and hauled off as green waste.

Hawaii banana tree

Bananas reproduce by creating baby trees at the base of the older tree. Just three banana trees turned into three massive clusters of dead, bug-infested banana tree stands. Our tiny garden created a truckload of green waste each week from huge palm leaves, dead banana trunks, rotten fruits, weeds, and dead flowers. Our yard was too small for a compost pile, which attracts bugs and rodents. The speed and height that trees and plants grow in Hawaii forced us to be judicious in how many we planted in our garden.

Some trees grow so huge in a tropical climate that it is hard for people coming from cold climates to grasp. Albizia trees, for example, are a fast growing tree that can block out the sun and kill other trees and plants. In Hawaii, they are considered a weed pest and dangerous due to their brittle wood and weak structure. Albizia trees grow to heights greater than 20 feet in the first year and up to 60 feet after ten years. We have friends in Puna on Hawaii Island whose single Albizia tree shades over a half an acre completely covering their house making cutting it down risky because it might crush their house if it falls the wrong way.

We were initially strongly against using herbicide because we were concerned about the environmental and health effects. We tried to control the weeds by pulling them by hand, but after a few months, our cars began to disappear behind the rapid growing weeds. Herbicide was the only defense we had against weeds and out of control grasses that took over our sidewalks and drains. We sprayed herbicide around the foundation perimeter of the house every week to control the growth and keep the weeds from filling in the crawlspace below the house. Even homes with lava fields as yards require some herbicide to keep weeds from overtaking the lava.

When planning your dream garden for your ideal home in Hawaii, consider the rapid growth, harvesting, and super height of flowers, trees, and bushes.

Bug and Pest Control in a Hawaii Garden

Hawaii chocolate (cacao) tree

The climate in Hawaii is as delightful to bugs and pests as it is to people and they are a part of living around lush tropical gardens. We have found that living in harmony with the bugs and pests in Hawaii and managing their population in the garden and grounds around the house is a more sane approach than being in constant conflict with them or hopelessly trying to eradicate them.

Bugs can be destructive or beneficial to a garden. Some bugs improve the soil or pollinate the plants. Bees, for example, are declining in number in Hawaii and yet a necessity for flowers and fruits.

On our return from a trip out of town, we found an entire bee swarm attached to a tree next to our house. Though we were not happy about having our yard taken over by the bees, killing them was unthinkable. We called an apiary, a beekeeper, in Puna and he was very pleased to drive into Hilo to come and get them. He arrived at dusk when the swarm was quieter and more tightly compacted. He set a large dark tarp down on the ground and a beehive box on top right under the tree branch with the majority of the swarm where the queen bee was most likely located. He cut the branch and gently set it on top of the box causing the bees to slowly slide off the branch into the box. Finally, he covered the box with the tarp, loaded them in his truck and drove off.

bee swarm in Hilo

Although tight fitting screens over the windows and good airflow can help discourage bugs from moving inside the house, bugs cannot be avoided when outside. Hawaii has biting mosquitoes that live year round, some that bite during the day and some at night. Mosquitoes lay hundreds of eggs at a time in even small amounts of standing water found in gutters, old tires, or even leaves of a bromeliad. We have had larvae appear in a flower vase that sat on our dining room table for a couple of weeks. Mosquitoes are something to take seriously since tropical diseases can spread by their bites. Although Hawaii has never had malaria or yellow fever, there are cases of dengue fever and West Nile virus. In some places in Hawaii, mosquitoes are constantly present and people wear long pants and sleeves for protection. Some natural pesticides are helpful like Neem oil and oil of lemon eucalyptus, but DEET is the most popular pesticide used to keep off the mosquitoes while working in the garden.

We have tried non-pesticide options, such as soapy water on fruit trees and planting bug resistant plants to help keep bugs under control, but the variety and amount of bugs in the Hawaii climate has required that we use pesticides for some bug infestations. Bugs like aphids, whitefly, scales, leafhoppers, and mealy bugs are common and create a sugary substance, which attracts ants and causes mold fungus, which ultimately kills the plant. Slugs and snails feed at night on bark, leaves, and fruits and hide during the day under boards, rocks, potted plants, and dirt. Traps, pheromone baits, screens and nets, collars around seedlings, and coating tree trunks are some of the ways to control pests. The state of Hawaii has set up controls to restrict the movement of plants around the state to help prevent the spreading of insects. The state of Hawaii and the EPA control insecticides and environmental friendly versions are the most desirable with moderate usage.

If you want to grow fruit or vegetables in your garden, then controlling bugs and rodents is important because of potential health dangers caused by pests contaminating the produce. For example, slug larvae hidden in vegetables have transmitted rat-lungworm to people who ate it raw. Rat-lungworm is a tropical disease caused by a parasitic worm carried by rats. Snails and slugs eat the feces of rats with worm larvae and hide in lettuce, peppers, and other produce. Rat-lungworm can cause meningitis and even coma in bad cases and physical discomfort at a minimum.

A sudden pest invasion can interfere with a planned coffee or chocolate crop in your garden. The coffee berry borer, for example, has shown up in Kona and restricted the movement of coffee berries grown on Hawaii Island. In Hawaii, pest invasions are common due to the tropical climate and influx of people, animals, produce, and plants from all over the world. Besides bugs and rodents, Hawaii has loud birds, wild pigs, deer, and other species problematic to gardens.

Kona coffee plant with ripening cherries

Genetically modified (GMO) fruits and vegetables are under development in Hawaii to deal with pests. Today, the majority of papayas grown in Hawaii are from seeds genetically altered to deal with pests that wiped out the crop in Oahu and on the island of Hawaii years ago. Not everyone agrees that eating fruits and vegetables genetically altered to contain pesticides is safe, but whether you are pro or anti GMO, you may want to know in advance of buying a property what varieties of fruits and vegetables are already growing on it.

Hawaii papayas

Planning for and controlling parasites, rodents, and bugs in a garden or acreage takes a concerted effort of trapping, poisoning, and clearing brush and weeds. Understanding the types of insects and the extent of any pest infestation in a garden that you are considering buying is an important part of evaluating a property in Hawaii.

Chapter Three
Buying or Building in Hawaii

Hawaii's Volatile Real Estate Prices

Most people that move to Hawaii hope to own a home on one of the islands. Because of Hawaii's central location in the Pacific Ocean, real estate prices are driven by factors like currency exchange rates in Asia and Europe, and economic cycles in Japan and Canada. The prices of properties in Hawaii have experienced big ups and downs completely unrelated to the economic situation on the mainland US. In the early 1990s, when Japan's economy went into a downturn, luxury condominium prices in Kona took a plunge and to this day some still sell for less than half of what they did in the 1970s. Hawaii's real estate market has historically been highly volatile and very wealthy people have misjudged the real estate market and lost staggering sums of money investing in it.

In the past decade, the real estate bubble on the mainland led to big price increases in real estate on the islands driven by mainland speculators. Since the US real estate bubble burst, prices in Hawaii have dropped steadily and many of the houses and condos on the islands are now being listed for considerably less than what they sold for in 2008. Whether or not real estate prices have hit bottom, timing is always an important part of the buying or building decision in Hawaii. If you can time your building project to a downturn in the cycle, you will find more building crews available for work. If you can time your home purchase to a down-cycle, you will have a substantially better selection of properties with significantly better prices.

Hawaii's climate and landscape make it a unique place in the US and the available land on the islands will always be limited. The inherent value of Hawaii real estate means prices for land, houses, and condominiums could suddenly soar for any number of reasons. Seventy-seven million US baby boomers are just starting to reach retirement age and if only 200,000, just ¼ of 1%, of those boomers decide to retire in Hawaii, real estate could instantly become a scarce commodity. If immigration laws change and make it easier for Asians to move to Hawaii, it could drive prices back to where they were in the 1970s. On the other hand, if Hawaii's population decreases or the Asian economy crashes, real estate prices might continue downward for some time.

Though the volatility of the island's real estate prices has meant large paper losses for most owners, as it has for us, we believe that the benefits of owning property in Hawaii outweigh any downside of the price drops. Owning real estate in paradise is a dream come true for us and the downturn in prices has not changed our view of the value or joy of our property ownership in Hawaii.

Buying a Home in Hawaii

neighborhood on Oahu

When you buy a house or condominium in Hawaii, you are choosing a lifestyle and a community. If you pick a neighborhood with newer mainland style houses, for example, you will likely be moving into an area with other newcomers to the island making living in Hawaii more like the mainland. If you move to an old Hawaii town like Hilo or Makaha however, it may feel more like living in a foreign country and some of your neighbors may not even speak English.

If you buy an older Hawaii home, a detailed inspection will reveal the extent of damage from bugs, mold, and mildew, which may be hard to detect. This is true on the mainland as well, however, in Hawaii damage from bugs and humidity is often more extensive. Buying a property, "as is" can mean taking on an impossible mold or pest infestation. We have friends with decades of experience buying older homes, fixing them up, and selling them at a good profit on the mainland. The extent of the damage from tropical mold in their Hawaii house was beyond anything they had experienced and their "mainland fixing for profit" real estate method turned into an expensive lesson in how Hawaii's real estate problems are different.

Typical mainland-style tract housing is also available on the islands, often from well-known mainland builders. Some of these builders bring in mainland crews for their housing projects to replicate the construction techniques they use elsewhere. Unfortunately, these builders often use designs that are not suited for the weather in Hawaii. Mainland-style house designs tend to sell well to new arrivals to Hawaii familiar with the look and feel, but the houses tend to use a lot of electricity to keep cool and often are not well suited for the rainfall, humidity, and bugs of Hawaii's tropical climate.

Many places in Hawaii have limited infrastructure for houses and condominiums. As a result, builders often install roads, sewer services, and even water systems as a part of their housing developments. These utilities become the responsibility of a homeowners association to manage and keep in compliance once the builder exits. This type of localized infrastructure is an important part of the affordability and livability of a house or condominium in Hawaii. Some condominiums provide all the utilities, even electric and cable services, while others provide only some and you are on your own to provide any other infrastructure or utilities. Individual properties in remote areas may have a well, water catchment system, septic system, solar system or other wholly contained off-the-grid utilities. Assessing utilities adds complexity to a home inspection when purchasing a house or condominium.

Renting in the area you are interested in is a good way to get a feel for the community you are considering. The neighbors, shopping, activities, beaches and many other aspects are unique on each island and in each town in Hawaii. Unlike the mainland, there are not many news sources or statistics about the activities, crimes, or actual weather in a given area in Hawaii, particularly on the outer islands. Renting is really the only way to find out in advance what it is really like to live there before taking the risk of ending up in a place you do not like. Everyone we have met that is happy in their Hawaii home rented in the area first.

Building a House in Hawaii

house construction in Hawaii

One of the benefits of building your own house in Hawaii is that you have a choice in the location of the property and it can cost less than a pre-built house. Building a house allows you to design it with your favorite Hawaii design elements and position it for the best view and to maximize airflow. Utility costs can be minimized in advance by installing solar systems, specifying LED lights, and harmonizing the house with the tropical environment.

One of the challenges of building a house in Hawaii is that key structural components and hardware shipped in from the mainland are hard to replace if they get broken or are missing from the primary shipping container. We met an owner builder with all the materials for his mainland-designed house shipped from Seattle to Hawaii. He calculated that it would save him $8000 over buying the materials locally. During construction, a damaged prefabricated roof truss delayed his house construction project six weeks while the crew waited for shipment of a replacement component from a lumber mill in Seattle. That was not his only delay. When it came time to put the roof on, he discovered that the specialty nails required had not been ordered and since they were not available in Hawaii, he had to have them air freighted over from the mainland.

Another challenge when building in Hawaii is getting skilled construction workers. Highly skilled construction workers are in short supply and the competition for them is high. Some house builders find it more affordable to fly in a crew from the mainland to do the project. This guarantees that a crew is only working on your house rather than other projects and they are less likely to abandon work when the surf is up. Knowing the capabilities of the construction crew helps to assure they follow the design, use the right materials, and properly install pre-fabricated sections. Unions have a lot of power in Hawaii and there have been cases where dockworkers have refused to unload a container with building supplies until the builder agrees to hire local union members. When you make your house-building project positive for local workers as well as your new neighbors, it goes a long way toward making your life in Hawaii more enjoyable and fun.

Hawaii has other building challenges as well. Since concrete has to be imported to Hawaii, it is more expensive and slabs are often poured thin as compared to the mainland. In areas near the ocean with constant sea spray the rebar in concrete rusts and the concrete can fall off around the rust. Drilling into lava to create ditches for water or sewer lines under a concrete slab is very challenging and expensive. These factors have led many in Hawaii to prefer post and pier construction to concrete foundations.

Security is an issue when building a house in Hawaii as theft of construction materials is very common. There is even a term for houses built with stolen materials in Hawaii; it is called a "found house" meaning "I found a little of it here and a little of it there". Security is even more challenging if the house is being built in a remote area. Our building project in Kau district of Hawaii Island ended when we were advised by several builders that before they would consider giving us a proposal to build a kit house we had selected, a plan for the security of the materials would have to be worked out. Several proposals were made to resolve the issue. One idea was to get a trailer or camper so we could live there for the duration of the construction. Another suggestion was to first build an Ohana, a small one bedroom house at the front of the property, so that someone could live there to provide the needed security for the house during the construction. Providing security during building can erase some of the cost benefits of building versus buying a house in Hawaii.

Using pre-manufactured floor trusses is far cheaper than traditional materials and they are lighter and easier for construction workers to assemble. The trusses have built in spaces to string utilities so there is no need to drill holes to put in electricity, plumbing, and air conditioning, which weakens the structure. The Wood Truss Council of America reports that the use of floor framing trusses in construction saves 26 hours of labor for floor installation and over 1000 board feet of lumber. Roof truss framing saves 83 hours and over 2000 board feet for a second floor and 68 hours and over 1500 board feet for a great-room. However, they base these savings in labor using building crews with a lot of experience installing prefabricated structures. Without this experience, installation of the units may be faulty making floors excessively squeaky and the building less secure during a hurricane or earthquake.

Building your ideal home in Hawaii may be the best choice if you can deal with the unique construction issues, material availability, delivery challenges, permitting processes, and work environment in Hawaii.

Building a Hawaii House Kit

Building a Hawaii-style house kit is one way to minimize the cost of materials and make sure the house is appropriate for Hawaii's climate. Using a local Hawaii house kit resolves the problem of long delays for building supplies from the mainland because the parts and replacement parts are stored locally.

Local crews are less versed in some of the mainland house building techniques and installation of pre-fabricated trusses from the mainland, but they have a high level of skill in building the popular Hawaii house kit models. They can offer valuable advice about how to configure a model to meet your needs. For example, the model may be built with higher interior walls to get more airflow, the master bathroom may be expanded into the space of one of the bedrooms, and the deck material for the porch may be upgraded. The Hawaii-style house kits use design elements such as large lanais, long overhanging eaves, and take into consideration Hawaii's trade winds. These features keep the house cooler, conserve on electricity, and make sense for Hawaii's tropical weather.

Hawaii building supply outlets, like HPM, have blueprints and carry all the supplies for Hawaii-style house kits. These house plans seem to get approval for building permits with less delay because the permit committee members have seen the blueprints so frequently. The designs use common building techniques like post and pier construction and hip-style, metal roofs. The materials are pre-specified and local so the houses go up quickly without unexpected problems or shortages of critical materials. Reducing the construction time can save on the cost of alternative housing during construction, the cost of gas if the crew is commuting from another area, and the need for security to watch the building supplies during construction.

The cost of building a house kit can vary depending on how much of the work you do yourself. In one case we know of, a family with two teenage boys built a 1350 square foot HPM house kit in 60 days. They claimed their cost of construction, excluding living expenses, was $42,000, which was primarily the cost of the house kit at that time. This did not include the costs of a water catchment system, septic system, connecting to electric, driveway, or added garage. It did include several upgrades to the materials used for the large lanai and kitchen counter tops. It may not be a typical scenario as the Dad and his sons had some minor building experiences, but the house turned out great even though it was the family's first attempt at building a kit.

To use a local contractor to build a house kit is significantly more costly than building it yourself. Contractors include the cost of round the clock security, labor costs of their crew, fuel costs of getting their crew back and forth to the building site, and their cost of management, risk and profit. Building a kit yourself or even living on the site to provide security and support can make a huge difference in defraying the costs of the construction. House kits have gone up in price due to increases in the cost of materials and fuel, but they still provide a more affordable way to build a house in Hawaii.

Chapter Four
Costs of Home Ownership

High Cost of Utilities in Hawaii

 When we opened up our first electric bill in Hawaii, we were sure that it was a mistake. It was over $450 and we were used to paying about $100 in northern California. We had used almost the exact same amount of electricity in kilowatt-hours, but it was over four times more expensive. We have made it a point since then to find as many ways as possible to save on our use of electricity.

Electricity is expensive in Hawaii because the products used to feed the power plants on the islands, like oil, diesel, naphtha, and coal are all shipped thousands of miles to Hawaii. The electricity needed for each island must be generated on that island, which adds to the cost. The power plants have to handle the maximum load when tourists fill the hotels and turn on the air conditioners as well as operate with a minimal load during off-season and sometimes shut down entirely. The economies of scale that big power plants have on the mainland do not apply to Hawaii's small and inefficient power plants and the residents pay for it with substantially higher electric bills.

The state of Hawaii has been proactive about encouraging renewable sources of energy. To encourage investment in green energy projects, the state passed a law that made it mandatory for Hawaii's electric utility company to pay oil-based costs for renewable sources of electricity. That drew in investors willing to spend money on Hawaii Island to provide power from geothermal, wind, solar and hydroelectric. The result is that on Hawaii Island over 40% of the island's electricity is from renewable sources. The downside of tying electric contracts to the price of oil has meant that residents and businesses are paying dearly for these alternative forms of energy production. Oahu Island has more low cost coal and other power plants without the alternative energy contracts, which mean residents of Oahu are charged 30% less than residents of outer islands for electric services and this difference increases whenever oil prices escalate. In 2008, the state of Hawaii signed an energy agreement to decouple energy costs from fossil fuel prices for renewable energy contracts, but existing contracts guarantee high returns for 10 to 15 more years. Below are two residential electric bills in March 2011 from condominiums in Kona and Honolulu:

Honolulu:
355 kilowatt hours = $112.35
Non-fuel energy (labor and maintenance) $27.14
Base fuel energy $32.20
Public Benefits Fund (pbf) surcharge $2.11
Overall $.316 per KWH

Kona:
413 kilowatt hours = $175.98
 Non-fuel energy (labor and maintenance) $53.33

 Base fuel energy $69.17
 Public Benefits Fund (pbf) surcharge $2.45
Overall $.426 per KWH

To minimize our energy costs we conserve electricity as much as possible. We rarely run the air conditioner, because it can add hundreds of dollars to an electric bill every month. We replaced all our incandescent light bulbs with compact florescent bulbs and are starting to use LED lights. We bought a device that displays how many kilowatts an appliance is using and found that many of our appliances use power even when they are not in use, like our exercise bicycle, DVD player, and coffee pot. Now we keep everything unplugged when not being used. We use cold water in our washing machine and open the dishwasher to dry rather than let it dry with heated air, which uses more electricity. All these changes dropped our electricity bill over 50%. When we later moved to a rental with a newer, energy efficient refrigerator, washer, and dryer, we were able to cut our electric bill back another 25%.

Installing an alternative energy system such as a solar water heater and solar electric panels would make an even more dramatic difference and potentially mean no electric bill. Fortunately, the cost of solar systems has dropped considerably making it faster to gain a return on the investment for a home based system. The state of Hawaii passed a law requiring all new houses to have solar energy hot water systems, which addresses one of the largest usages of electricity in the home.

Water service is expensive in Hawaii because it requires electricity to pump it to housings high above sea level from the lava rock where it collects from rainfall. Most water bills in Hawaii show the cost of electricity used each month.

On the outer islands, water services are not available everywhere. Drilling for water in lava rock is expensive and ground water does not exist in some areas. As a result, many residential properties rely on rainwater catchment systems. These systems require maintenance of one or more large water tanks to minimize rust and holes and keep rodents and bugs from getting inside. During some times of the year, the water tanks dry out from lack of rain so residents rely on water trucks to refresh their systems with water. The high acidity of the rain from volcanic emissions, particularly on the island of Hawaii, makes drinking rainwater unsafe. Drinking water must be hauled in from community water taps or store bought if you have a catchment system or if the well water is not safe. We know many people that bought in remote areas and did not calculate the cost of buying drinking water and the fuel to haul it in, much less the expense of keeping their water catchment tanks clean when buying their home.

In Hawaii most of the water looks and tastes great, however it sometimes has high salt and calcium content and can be very acidic. A water filtration system is highly advisable to improve the water and protect the pipes and plumbing. Even with a filtration system, we still depend on bottled drinking water.

Sewer costs are high in Hawaii because they are tied to the volume of water consumed. The cost of treating wastewater is also high. Many residential communities, apartments, and even commercial buildings have shared sewer systems installed by the builders, which the owners are responsible for maintaining and keeping in federal compliance. We know of million dollar homes that share a small sewer system with a dozen other homes in an upscale part of Kona. This adds potential complexity to owning a house and it is worth finding out in advance what expertise the homeowners are using to keep the system running smoothly.

Houses in Hawaii have more cesspools than any other state in the US, and they discharge raw, untreated sewage directly into the ground and can contaminate the ocean and ground water by releasing disease-causing pathogens and nitrates. These cesspools have been out of EPA compliance since 2005 and if not replaced with new systems the owners risk getting a fine from the county, state or federal government. Many buyers are not aware at the time of their purchase that the property is out of compliance with the EPA and they end up taking on the fines and having to clean up and reinstall a new system. Since city sewer facilities are not widely available on the outer islands of Hawaii, paying for a private sewage system is often an unexpected cost.

Fees and Taxes on Hawaii Property

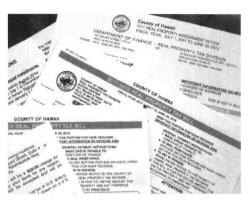

It may sound odd but we were excited when we got our first property tax bill from Hawaii County. It was no longer a question of if we were moving to Hawaii, only a question of when. In the decade since we bought our property, we watched real estate prices soar along with our property taxes, and then drop back to almost what we originally paid. Each county in the state of Hawaii bases their property taxes on the assessed fair market value. Reassessments of properties are prompt as prices increase or decline as compared to other states we have lived in, perhaps because Hawaii has had a lot of practice at boom and bust real estate cycles.

Each county has their own tax rate structure for the classes of properties that they have defined such as: residential, commercial, commercialized residential, affordable rental housing, conservation, industrial, agriculture, vacant agriculture, preservation, resort, timeshare, apartment, etc. The counties give substantial tax relief to owners that reside in the home as a principal residence and owners over age 65. There are also tax exemptions for disabled veterans, owners that are confined with Hansen's disease, blind, deaf, or totally disabled. Recently the counties have been raising their tax rates to cover for

43

drops in property tax revenue from lower assessed values. Any loss in property taxes has an immediate effect on every county budget in the state because it is their largest source of revenue.

Property tax bills are mailed out once a year in August and the taxes can be paid in one payment or two (August and February). Current and historic tax information is available for every property online on websites managed by each county at www.(*countyname*)propertytax.com. You can view the tax bill and owner information for any property using the unique Hawaii Tax Map Key (TMK) code assigned to every property in Hawaii.

Any water, sewer, or road infrastructure as well as shared grounds, facilities and garbage services set up for a subdivision or condominium by the original land developer or builder is usually turned over to a home owners association or maintenance corporation. These organizations are funded from monthly or annual fees from the owners. In some condominium complexes, monthly fees include all the utilities including water, sewer, garbage, electric, cable, and grounds maintenance. If the grounds of a housing or condominium complex are large, then gardening fees, water, lighting, facilities, and management fees can be substantial. An owners association can be highly political with big budgets and intense legal disputes between different groups of owners demanding their favorite manager or landscaping company or contractor be hired costing the association hundreds of thousands or millions a year.

Condominium units in foreclosure may pay no owner fees for years and since Hawaii law limits the amount of recovery, the other owners end up covering these costs. Many communities charge fees based on the square footage of the unit, particularly if utilities are included. As a result, fees can be vastly different from one unit to another in the same complex, which makes it important to verify the fee for the specific unit or house rather than assume every unit has a similar fee. New owners may have to pay any fees owed by the previous owners that were not settled as a part of a foreclosure or short sale. If the fees are not paid, the owner's organization can put a lien against the property and in some cases sell it to pay for the fees. We know of undeveloped properties that were taken from their owners for unpaid annual road maintenance fees of less than $100.

Homeowner fees can vary greatly from one residential complex to the next. On the island of Hawaii, there are resort communities that charge over $4,000 a month for full time security guards, a fancy beach club, golf membership, road and grounds maintenance, and other amenities. Down the road, another almost identical residential complex charges less than half of that. Though tropical grounds with pools and a hot tub are very appealing, very few residents regularly use them. However, keeping a hot tub at 100 degrees Fahrenheit can cost over $2000 a month and lighting around the complex can be equally expensive. Even small condominium complexes usually have at least one full time manager to deal with the many tasks required to maintain the property and the peace among the residents. Having a manager attuned to conserving water and electricity and closely managing contractors can save the owners a lot of money as well as keeping the association from raising the fees whenever there is an increase in utility prices.

gated community in Hawaii

Older condominiums may decide to upgrade or refurbish their building exteriors or facilities. If a condominium complex cannot pay for an upgrade or refurbishment from their existing balance, they charge a special assessment fee to the owners. Realtors may not know or may gloss over an impending upgrade, which can mean a large, one-time charge for the unit. In addition to the cost, it can be a real pain to live in a construction zone or have the pool unavailable while the improvements are being made. One condominium complex in Kona assessed their owners $60,000 each for a major upgrade to the building, which was more than many of the owners paid for their units when they were new. A telltale sign that an assessment might be on the horizon is when an older complex has a sudden surge in the number of units for sale after years of low turnover.

Insurance Costs in Hawaii

We have used the same insurance company that we signed up with out of high school over 35 years ago. No matter where we have lived or purchased property, they were always able to add it to our policy, until we moved to Hawaii. Suddenly, we had to find a new insurance company to cover our property insurance because they considered it too risky to insure. Hawaii has tsunamis, earthquakes, lava flows, volcanic eruptions, floods, hurricanes, and wild fires. We were able to find another insurance company, one that specializes in Hawaii property, but our policies are three times higher than we ever paid on the mainland. Higher insurance can be a surprise cost of ownership in Hawaii.

Tsunami zones, lava flow zones, and spotty police and fire department coverage in remote areas complicate Hawaii's property insurance coverage. A house may not be eligible for flood insurance because of its location inside a tsunami zone or flood zone. There was tsunami damage on all the islands due to the massive earthquake in Japan, particularly on Hawaii Island and Oahu. However, nearby landslides can also cause tsunamis and flooding at sea level. Flooding can also be a problem in low-lying areas from heavy rains, even in dry parts of Hawaii.

Hawaii County properties are in one of nine lava zones based on the assessed risk of new lava flows. The greatest hazard is Lava zone 1, which includes areas around the volcanoes Kilauea and Mauna Loa where vents have been active. Properties in the first three zones have the greatest exposure and may have increase insurance costs or no insurance coverage available.

In remote areas with limited police coverage, there is an increased risk of robberies and insurance costs will reflect it. This is one way to find out how risky the insurance companies think a property is due to crime. Insurance companies also know if there are no fire stations nearby and reflect the risk in higher rates. Many remote areas are dependent are part-time volunteer firefighters with limited equipment to fight fires and respond to highway accidents.

Hurricane insurance and earthquake insurance are other additional insurance policies that are worth considering for houses in Hawaii. The majority of the destruction caused by Hurricane Iniki on Kauai was from the wind rather than the water so even houses far from the coast are at risk. Though Hawaii County has the most earthquakes, Maui and Oahu also have significant seismic activity and are at risk for earthquake damage.

Without insurance for a particular risk, it may be difficult to protect your Hawaii real estate investment, which may change your assessment of the value of the property.

Chapter Five
Hawaii's Unique Geography

The Chain of Islands in Hawaii

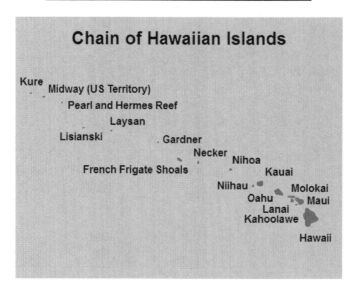

The Hawaiian Islands were formed from a geologic hot spot in the middle of the Pacific Ocean that has been erupting lava for the past 83 million years. As the Pacific plate moves over this spot, magma pushes through, creating new islands in the form of volcanoes. The Hawaiian Islands are just the uppermost crests of these volcanoes. The oldest islands, furthest from the hot spot, are slowly shrinking and eroding from rain, wind, ocean waves, and landslides while the youngest islands are still growing with new flows of lava. The Hawaiian Islands form an archipelago made up of 132 islands, atolls, shoals, and seamounts stretching 1523 miles from

Kure Atoll to Hawaii Island. Understanding Hawaii's unique island geography and topography helps in selecting a place to live that best fits your lifestyle and needs.

Of the eight main Hawaiian Islands, you can only live on six. Kahoolawe is controlled by the military and Niihau is privately owned. The older islands of Kauai and Oahu are flatter due to weather erosion while the newer islands of Maui and Hawaii have volcanoes that are so high they have arctic conditions at their summits. In Hawaii, everything from tropical white sand beaches, grass covered valleys, extreme deserts, rugged black lava beaches, tropical rainforests, and high altitude areas are available as home sites. Below are summaries of the six islands with residential properties in Hawaii.

The Island of Kauai

Kauai is the furthest north and tends to have the coolest temperatures at sea level. The island's interior is mountainous with steep canyons that are mostly uninhabited. Mount Kawaikini at 5245 feet and Mount Waialeale at 5148 feet are Kauai's highest points, remnants of once massive volcanoes. Mount Waialeale is considered one of the wettest spots on earth receiving an average of 480 inches of rain per year, which creates hundreds of waterfalls and rivers. The residents live mostly on the coastal plain on the southern side overlooking the beaches. The single main highway (Highway 50/56) connects Princeville on the northeastern side of the island to Mana Point on the western side, a distance of 65 miles. The northwestern portion of the island is inaccessible due to the sheer cliffs of the Napali Coast and the arid southwestern side of the island is mostly off-limits due to the Pacific Missile Range Facility.

Kauai County has less than 60,000 residents living in small towns along the highway. Rainfall along the populated coastal areas varies between 20 to 40 inches a year with more at the higher elevations. The island is slowly shrinking with Kauai's beaches disappearing at a rate of about one foot a year because of storms, waves, and chronic erosion of the aged and brittle lava.

If you are considering a move to Kauai, spend time there to see if the size, weather, and activities on the island match your lifestyle and needs. Though the channel between Oahu and Kauai is only 65 miles wide, you cannot jump in the car and drive to Honolulu; you have to fly to get there.

The Island of Oahu

The island of Oahu has the only incorporated city in the state, Honolulu, and the remainder of the island is designated as Honolulu County. The island is only 44

miles long and 30 miles wide and the center has remnants of two volcanoes, Waianae, with its tallest peak Mount Kaala at 4040 feet and Koolau with its highest point Konahuanui at 3150 feet. Giant chunks of Oahu are strewn on the ocean floor northeast of the island from avalanches and landslides in the past. Oahu's beaches are eroding and the island has lost nearly 17 miles of its sandy shoreline since the 1940s due to erosion and wave action.

Oahu is home to most of the state's population, at 963,200 in 2011, as well as about 5 million visitors a year. The island has a significant military presence with numerous bases employing almost 50,000 military personnel. The acreage set aside for military bases, forest reserves, and other lands off-limits greatly restricts the amount of residential property and building sites available on the island. Though it is a small island, Oahu has the most activities, hotels, entertainment, schools, and jobs, in Hawaii. It also has the most crime, crowding, and traffic jams.

The Islands of Maui, Lanai, and Molokai

Maui County encompasses three islands, Maui, Lanai, and Molokai. These islands, along with the island of Kahoolawe were once a single island with six volcanoes, similar in size to the island of Hawaii.

53

Maui is the largest and most populated island in the county and the second largest island in the state. Haleakala Volcano rises to 10,020 feet and has been dormant since 1790. The island of Maui has dramatic differences in landscapes and climates due to the altitude and the different orientations toward the trade winds. The population on the island is about 140,000 with over 2 million visitors each year. Maui has a big selection of unique places to live with white sandy beaches at sea level and numerous towns and residential areas at different elevations on the tropical side and dry side of the two volcanoes providing a wide range of choices in views, climates, and vegetation. Maui's main drawback for many people is that the cost of living is substantially more expensive when compared to the other islands.

The island of Lanai is only 13 miles wide with the highest point of 3370 feet above sea level. Lanai used to be owned by Dole Pineapple and a single company still owns and controls 98% of the island. As a result, the population on Lanai is only about 3000 residents with their livelihoods mostly centered on the resorts.

The island of Molokai is only 10 miles wide at its widest point and almost 40 miles long. The highest points are Puu Nana, at 1380 feet, on the dry west end, and Kamakou at 4,970 feet on the east end of the island. The north shore Pali has the tallest sea cliffs in the world created when half of the island slid into the ocean from an avalanche. The island has a tight knit community of about 7000 residents. Housing options are limited on the island and there is little in the way of shopping and city-type activities. If you are looking for remoteness, great views, and a beautiful white sand beach this island may be worth considering.

The Island of Hawaii

The island of Hawaii is the largest in the state, over twice the size of all the other islands combined and yet the population is only about 180,000. Because it is the furthest south and has the highest volcanoes, it has the warmest and coldest temperatures in the state. Two volcanoes dominate the island, Mauna Kea, which rises to 13,796 feet and Mauna Loa almost as tall at 13,676 feet. These volcanoes separate the very moist east side of the island from the drier west side. Highways go around the island, except for the Puna coast on the southeastern side, which is cut off by lava flows into the ocean. Saddle Road, a highway between Mauna Kea and Mauna Loa, connects the two sides of the island and rises to an altitude of 6600 feet. At the top of Saddle Road is a Military training area and Mauna Kea Summit Road, which provides access to the international telescopes up on the summit of Mauna Kea.

We picked the island of Hawaii as our home because of the diversity of landscapes, climate, activities, and residential communities as well as having the lowest cost of living in the state. The island is less touristy than Oahu and Maui and more devoted to farming, fishing, and livestock production. Resort hotels are clustered in the small arid zone of the western Kohala coast with white sand beaches. The majority of the population lives on the tropical east side of the island where there is excellent farming and fishing

Kilauea Volcano on Hawaii Island

Risks of Living on the Slopes of a Volcano

Lava and Vog

The island of Hawaii has five volcanoes, Kohala, Mauna Kea, Kilauea, Mauna Loa, and Hualalai with all but Kohala still active. Residential properties in the districts of Kau and Puna have the highest possibility of being covered by new lava flows on the island. The area surrounding Kailua-Kona is also at risk for lava flows because it is on the slopes of Hualalai Volcano, which last erupted in 1801 and is overdue for an eruption.

Kilauea Volcano has been erupting almost continuously for over 30 years, pouring lava into the ocean and puffing out thousands of tons of sulfur dioxide and poisonous gasses every day. These volcanic emissions, called "vog" or volcanic smog, vary based on the volcano's daily activity. Some people have a bad reaction to the vog with burning eyes, sore throats, chest tightening and asthma attacks. We are lucky that we do not have a bad reaction, but on heavy vog days, we stay inside and run the air conditioner to dry out the air, which helps remove the irritating sulfur dioxide. Though the island of Hawaii has the most vog, when the trade winds stop blowing, vog spreads to Maui and Oahu.

Earthquakes and Tsunamis
Historically tsunamis in Hawaii have been deadly and destructive. Many areas destroyed by tsunamis in the past are now grass filled parks. The early warning alarm systems on the islands alert most residents in

time for them to get to higher ground before a tsunami generated by a large earthquake on a distant continent hits Hawaii. Although you might think these events are rare, in our four years in Hawaii we have helped a business evacuate their products from a tsunami zone and been evacuated from our home twice after distant earthquakes threatened Hawaii with a tsunami. On the evening of March 10, 2011, we packed up our car and spent the night parked in a shopping center lot at a higher elevation after sirens blared warning of a tsunami heading toward Hawaii. That tsunami, generated from a 9.0 earthquake in Japan, caused a lot of damage to homes, hotels, and docks along the coast of several islands in Hawaii.

Tsunamis are also created by a local earthquake, caused by the weight of the islands on the Pacific plate, or a chunk of an island crashing into the ocean. These tsunamis can come with no warning and because the event is so close, you have limited time to evacuate. In 1975, a section of Hilina Pali shelf on the banks of Kilauea volcano dropped into the ocean causing a 7.2 magnitude earthquake and a 48-foot tsunami, which killed 2 campers and injured 19 others. People here say if an earthquake knocks you off your feet, a tsunami is sure to follow and you should run as fast as you can to higher ground.

Island Fever
The remoteness of the Hawaiian Islands is not something to take lightly when considering a move. Hawaii is the most isolated population center in the world. It is 2,390 miles from the California coastline;

3,850 miles from Japan; 4,900 miles from China; and 5,280 miles from the Philippines. Many people that move to the islands overestimate how often family and friends will be able to visit. When we wake up in Hawaii, it is already afternoon on the East Coast of the US and the events of the day are mostly over. The physical remoteness and time differences from the mainland make living in Hawaii a very different reality.

Military bases, parks and other lands owned by the United States government comprise over 12% of Oahu and almost 20% of all the land in Hawaii. Much of the land on the islands is not accessible by roads due to the terrain or ownership by the military, federal government, Hawaii Homelands, and land trusts. The islands are cut off from each other by deep channels and a choppy ocean, so travel between the islands means flying. Only Oahu has much in the way of shopping or mainland style entertainment and restaurants. Getting restless or bored, known as "island fever", can become a significant issue for many that move to the islands.

Chapter Six
Hawaii's Varied Climate Zones

Hawaii's many Microclimates

Hawaii Island Climate Zones

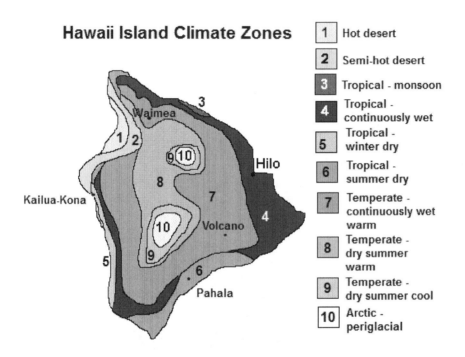

1	Hot desert
2	Semi-hot desert
3	Tropical - monsoon
4	Tropical - continuously wet
5	Tropical - winter dry
6	Tropical - summer dry
7	Temperate - continuously wet warm
8	Temperate - dry summer warm
9	Temperate - dry summer cool
10	Arctic - periglacial

Most people's first experience of Hawaii's climate is from staying at one of the beach resort areas like Waikiki on Oahu or the Kohala coast on the island of Hawaii or Wailea on Maui. These resorts are located in the dry, sunny part of the islands, but many of the residential areas in Hawaii are in wet, tropical climate zones. On the island of Hawaii, for example, only 445 full time residents live in the arid resort climate zone while the other 170,000 residents live in one of the tropical microclimate zones. We frequently meet people new to Hawaii that do not understand why it is so rainy where they moved compared to the weather they had during their vacation to the islands. Being aware of Hawaii's varied climate zones lets you choose the location that meets your preferences and weather expectations.

The climatologist Vladimir Köppen classified the world's climates into five zones: Tropical, Arid, Temperate, Cold-Continental, and Ice or Arctic. Hawaii is unique because it has four out of five of these dramatically different weather zones, all except the Cold-Continental zone. Other climatologists added sub-classifications or microclimates to each of the primary five climate zones. Guide books that boast Hawaii has 11 of the 13 climate zones are referring to microclimates within the four climate zones in Hawaii. The thing to realize is that the resorts in Hawaii are located in the driest climate zones on each island and beyond those few areas, there is the most incredible choice of tropical and temperate microclimates in the smallest area in the world. Very few places on earth get as much rainfall as the wettest parts of Hawaii or are as dry as the arid areas.

Hawaii's location in the Pacific Ocean gets consistent, moisture-laden winds, called the trade winds. Areas of the islands that face these trade winds get extraordinary rainfall whereas the leeward sides of the islands protected from the trade winds are drier with some areas that are arid, desert climates. Above sea level, the topography of the islands creates unique tropical and temperate microclimate zones up the slopes of the volcanoes. On the islands of Maui and Hawaii, the elevation of the volcanoes is so high that there are arctic climate zones at the top. The peaks, valleys, ridges, and slopes of the volcanoes create climatic variety within the islands by obstructing, deflecting, and accelerating the flow of air and small microclimates can exist with dramatically different rainfall and temperature differences within extremely short distances.

Each microclimate zone in Hawaii has its own unique eco-system, rainfall, humidity, wind flow, vegetation and even bugs. Just a few miles can mean the difference between a sunny, cool, dry, house versus a humid, stuffy, moldy, house. In some neighborhoods, just a few blocks can be the difference between a wet, tropical climate and a drier one.

<u>Choosing Your Microclimate</u>

summit of Mauna Kea Volcano

The dramatic differences between Hawaii's microclimates, makes the selection of a house or building site a choice of climate as well as a home. It helps put the climate differences in Hawaii into perspective to compare climate differences between Phoenix, Arizona and Eugene, Oregon two cities that are 1000 miles apart on the mainland with Hilo and Kawaihae two towns on the island of Hawaii only 60 miles apart. Phoenix is generally considered a desert with an average yearly rainfall of about 8 inches a year whereas Eugene is generally considered a rainy town with an average yearly rainfall of 50 inches, a difference of 42 inches between the two cities. In comparison, Kawaihae has an average yearly rainfall of 4 inches and Hilo has an average yearly rainfall of 130 inches. That is a difference of 125 inches of rainfall within 60 miles on Hawaii compared to the 42 inches of rainfall within a 1000 miles on the mainland.

If you visit a property on a bright sunny day, you may find it hard to believe that it rains almost continuously in that spot the rest of the year. The lava quickly absorbs standing water and the hot sun dries off the grasses and trees within hours. The few rain gauges located around the islands are not an accurate indication of rainfall or cloud cover for a particular location. We had over twice as much rain at our house in Hilo than the airport reported which was less than a mile away. Even slight changes in elevation, which face the trade winds, increase the amount of rain. Rainfall amounts are greatest between 2,000 to 3,000 feet above sea level and then decrease at the higher elevations. Each island in Hawaii varies in weather and rainfall in the areas that residential properties are available.

Kauai Rain Map

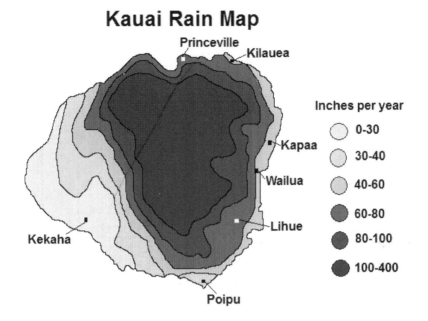

The island of Kauai has a narrow band where residential properties are located along the eastern and southern coasts. The arid western coast and the extreme rainy high elevations of the interior are not populated. Within the residential areas, the microclimate differences are primarily in amounts of rainfall, which varies substantially between the wetter eastern side and the dryer western side of the island. The towns on the northern side of the island near Princeville get up to 80 inches of rain a year as compared to the residential properties on the western side of the island near Kekaha, which get an average of 20 inches of rain.

Oahu Rain Map

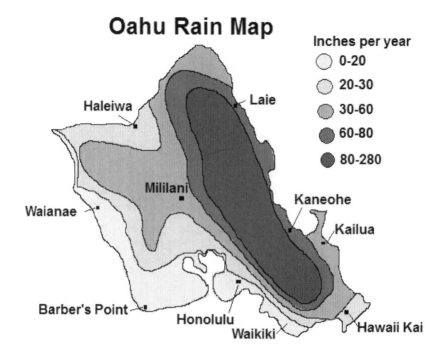

Inches per year
- ◯ 0-20
- ◔ 20-30
- ◕ 30-60
- ⬤ 60-80
- ⬤ 80-280

Haleiwa · Laie · Waianae · Mililani · Kaneohe · Kailua · Barber's Point · Honolulu · Waikiki · Hawaii Kai

The island of Oahu has large differences in rain and humidity with almost zero precipitation in some areas and up to 280 inches of rainfall a year in the interior of the island. Similar to Kauai, forest reserves, military bases and other lands off-limits to the public on Oahu restrict the actual climate zones where residential properties are generally available. The northeast coast of Oahu, along the Koolau Range, faces the trade winds, which creates lush vegetation with up to 80 inches of rainfall a year. In comparison, the western coast of Oahu is hot and dry because the Waianae Range shelters it from the trade winds. Most of Oahu's population lives along the southern coast of the island, which gets less than 20 inches of rain a year, but can vary in temperature depending on a particular area's access to trade winds.

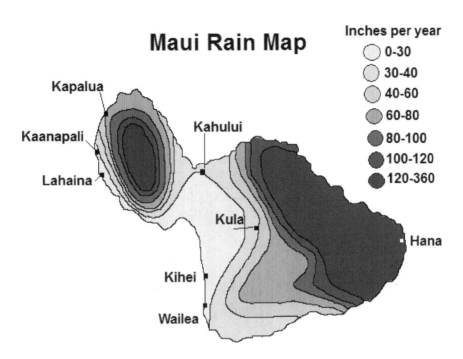

Maui Island has large differences in rainfall and temperatures in residential properties because of the island's irregular topography. The northern coast faces the trade winds, which makes it a favorite place for wind surfers, but also brings in cloud cover and rain. The interior of the island near Kahului and the airport, is drier with occasional rain in the afternoons. The resort hotels are located on the southern coasts at sea level where it is warm and dry. The amount of rainfall and cloud cover increases on Maui as the elevation increases up the slopes of the volcanoes.

The differences in climate on Maui can dominate the living experience in a town like Kula, which at an elevation of 3000 feet, is usually 10 to 20 degrees cooler than the towns at sea level below it.

67

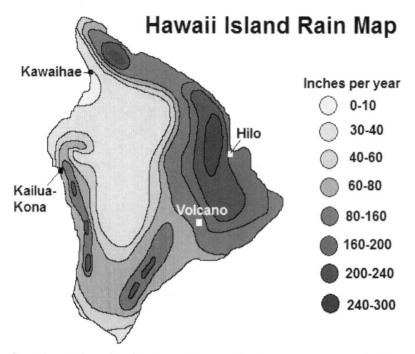

Hawaii Island Rain Map

Kawaihae

Hilo

Kailua-
Kona

Volcano

Inches per year
- 0-10
- 30-40
- 40-60
- 60-80
- 80-160
- 160-200
- 200-240
- 240-300

On the island of Hawaii, most of the residential areas are in tropical climate zones. The district of Puna, which is the size of Oahu, is mostly tropical rain forest as are the areas around Hilo. We have met many people that bought their piece of paradise in one of the Puna subdivisions after a vacation at a Waikoloa resort on the arid Kohala coast, shocked by the never-ending downpour of rain after they moved in. Newcomers from Oregon and Washington State, who think they are accustomed to a lot of rain, are dismayed at the rain like a fire-hose and high humidity of a rain forest compared to the drizzle and mist of the Pacific Northwest. The temperatures are cooler as the elevation increases up the slopes of the volcanoes, decreasing about 3 degrees every thousand feet.

In the winter, our friends that live at higher elevations above Hilo have to bundle up in thick coats and turn their car heater on high for the seven-mile drive down to the warm 80-degree morning in Hilo. While some are running their air conditioners to keep cool in downtown Hilo, a few miles above the town others are burning firewood to keep warm.

In the town of Waimea, one side of the town is wet and rainy most of the time while the other side of the town is dry with cactus growing. We often joke that if you bought a house in the right spot in that town you could have wet rainy climate on the back porch and a sunny, dry climate on the front porch.

In Kona, on the western coast, there are several bands of tropical microclimates up the slopes of Hualalai Volcano. The difference in elevation between just two streets in a residential community can mean being continuously under a thick cloud of mist or being in the sunlight. Kona's weather can be complicated by thick vog from the volcano that moves inland from the sea in the morning and rises up the slopes as the day heats up. During a heavy vog day, some areas of Kona are encased in a grey cloud while other areas are completely free of it.

Like all the islands in Hawaii, differences in climate within short distances make taking the time to understand the climate, wind, rainfall and humidity of a specific site well worth the effort.

Weather Cycles and Storms in Hawaii

Weather cycles and storms can change the temperature and rainfall in Hawaii, regardless of the climate zone. We have observed great variations in rainfall in Hawaii over the last four years. The most recent drought in Hawaii was attributed to an El Nino condition. An El Nino is a warming of the ocean temperature and causes hotter and drier winters in Hawaii. In 2008, the El Nino created drought conditions which became progressively worse until 2010. The green grasses covering Mauna Loa and Mauna Kea on Hawaii Island dried up, trees died, and it was hard for farmers and ranchers to keep their crops and livestock watered. At the time, we lived in Hilo and since it rained almost every day, we were amazed to find that the region was having a dry spell and getting less than 50% of the "normal rainfall". The weather has since changed and the increased rainfall is slowly recovering the green coat of grass on the slopes of Mauna Loa. This year Mauna Kea was covered with snow in June and sunny Kona has had noticeably more rain. La Nina conditions cause the opposite of an El Nino, making the trade winds stronger and the rain heavier than normal. When selecting a home with your ideal climate, make sure to find out if the area you are considering is having normal weather that year or is in a period of extreme dry or wet conditions.

Hurricanes can happen at any time in Hawaii, but they normally occur from June to November and they usually pass west or south of Hawaii. Unfortunately, when they do strike the damage can be epic. The most recent major hurricane to hit Hawaii was in 1992 and caused significant destruction on Kauai and other islands.

Hawaii's heaviest rains come from winter storms between October and April bringing frequent clouds as well as southerly and westerly winds. Hawaii often has flash floods from these storms and they are considered one of the most common weather hazards in the state. Waterspouts also occur in the winter months in Hawaiian waters and though they are usually mild, a few severe waterspouts have done destruction in the past.

Calculating the Value of good Weather

Most people that move to Hawaii focus on the price of the house and not the value of the weather where it is located. A house with year-round, sunny days next to a white sand beach will cost more than a house in a remote tropical rain forest. If you look at the home price from the perspective of the cost per day of ideal weather, the price may look very different. The key to finding an ideal Hawaii home is to look only in the areas with the type of climate you love.

We moved to Hawaii for the sunshine and the year-round, tropical weather. Though most things in Hawaii are more expensive than on the mainland US, we have found that the exceptional weather is saving us money in some unusual ways.

1. Reduced health care costs: The abundance of sunshine and the ease of swimming and getting exercise every day, year-round has improved our health. There is no ragweed season in Hawaii, which saves us months of misery, tissues, and the expense of allergy medicine. Having warm weather every day means less aches and pains in the morning and we no longer get colds and flus. We are saving on the cost of doctor visits and prescriptions. As our health improves, our savings could become even more substantial if it means we avoid heart disease, cancer, diabetes or any of the other chronic diseases of our time.
2. No need for vacations: We have not gone on a vacation in four years now because every day in Hawaii feels like a vacation and so far, we have no desire to ever leave the islands.
3. Greater availability and lower prices for fresh foods: The vegetables and fruits we like to eat are grown locally and cost less than what we paid on the mainland. The weather in Hawaii allows produce to grow year-round and it is available at farmer's markets and in local stores. Our local grass fed beef and fish are plentiful and substantially less expensive than on the mainland.
4. Reduced cost of heating and cooling: The weather is so moderate we rarely use air conditioning and heating is not required. We are saving money on heating and cooling. The cost of electricity is extremely high in Hawaii so these savings are not as substantial, however as

we invest in more energy efficient appliances and lighting our costs for electricity have continued to drop.

5. <u>Reduced cost of clothing:</u> We do not have to shovel snow in Hawaii or need coats, long johns, or special clothes for each season. In Hawaii's climate, we rarely wear shoes and live in T-shirts and shorts, so our clothes do not wear out as fast and are cheaper to replace. We do have to buy new bathing suits regularly because they wear out with everyday use. Overall, our clothing costs are substantially less than what we spent on the mainland.

After a couple of years of relaxing in the warm, laid-back, Hawaii atmosphere, we find that we need less space and temperatures that used to feel too hot to us now feel fine. After four years in Hawaii, we have changed so much that we can now live in warmer climates and smaller residences.

We initially moved to Hilo and it felt hot and humid to us compared to where we moved from in northern California. We kept cool by swimming daily, which lowered our body temperature. After two years in Hilo, the winters began to feel so "cold" to us that we could no longer swim year round. We moved to Kailua-Kona, which has a dry winter and is warmer and sunnier. Kona, which we thought was too hot when we first arrived in Hawaii, is now the perfect temperature for us and we can swim year round.

Chapter Seven
Hawaii's Tropical Environment

Life on a Tropical Island

We first lived in the tropics while in high school on the island of Java. We loved the tropics, the warm days, comfortable nights, and the daylight hours staying the same all year. The exotic fruits were a constant delight as were the delicious fish, shrimp, and lobster. The pace was slow and people were friendly. It was a place where we both flourished, our extra weight came off, our acne was replaced with tans, and the humidity felt great on our skin.

Living in the tropics had its challenges, however, like the heavy rains that washed black-spitting cobras off the roofs on to sidewalks and toxic caterpillars that hid in the bushes. Our hikes in the rainforests usually required the removal of large leeches and we had to share the beaches with poisonous sea snakes. Massive swarms of termites in the house would block out the view of the other side of the room and an army of ants would instantly appear to eat any food left out by mistake. The rats in an open drainage pipe in the backyard were the size of big dogs and our house was sometimes surrounded by thousands of cute mini-toads that had poison stingers on their tongues. We came to dread the upset stomachs we got from taking quinine to ward off malaria and we had to endure tropical diseases that the doctors never could identify.

We love living in Hawaii because it offers the benefits of a tropical climate without the hazards we faced in Java. Newcomers to Hawaii, who have never lived in the tropics, can find it challenging to deal with the bugs, rodents, and molds that can overtake your home. Spiders, beetles, slugs, creepy crawling things, loud frogs, and other critters thrive in Hawaii's great weather just like we do. However, Hawaii has no venomous snakes, frogs or caterpillars. Only one type of centipede is poisonous and although the gigantic cockroaches are scary when they fly at you, they are not dangerous. Compared to living in Java, Hawaii's tropical challenges seem minor to us and having the rights and benefits of being a citizen in a US state is no small thing in our experience. This chapter briefly describes some of the pests in Hawaii that we think are useful to know about before selecting a location or home in Hawaii.

Tropical Bugs

centipede

Ordinary Ants, Extraordinary Pests

Hawaii has over forty varieties of ants, however, the pharaoh ant and the thief ant cause the most problems in Hawaii homes.

Pharaoh ants, from Africa, thrive year round in the warm ground in Hawaii producing a never ending stream of new ant colonies. As soon as you get rid of a colony, there are five new ones to replace them. Spraying insecticide can make the problem worse, because it causes the ant colonies to "bud". Budding is when the colonies mass-produce new queens to start new colonies. A few days after a pesticide spraying at our condominium complex, the grounds are filled with flying ant queens and a few weeks later we notice trucks from pest control companies, the drivers with big smiles, arriving to spray individual units. The best approach for controlling pharaoh ants is to put poison baits around the outside perimeter of your home. It helps to have poison baits inside as well for the ants that manage to get through the perimeter. If you do not have control over the outside of your house, as is common in condominium complexes, putting fresh baits out right after the grounds are sprayed will help deal with the new influx of ants.

Because they look similar, thief ants live off of pharaoh ant colonies by going into their colonies and stealing their food. When pharaoh ant colonies are destroyed by poison baits, the thief ants show up around the house looking for a new source of food.

Unlike pharaoh ants, thief ants can be killed with spraying. Poison baits are not effective on thief ants because their colonies are small and they do not feed off a single source long enough to be affected by the poison.

Tropical Termites

After moving into a house in Hilo, we found piles of black dirt in drawers and shelves that looked like coffee grounds. It took us a while to figure out that this material, called flit, was a sign that the house had termites. The house was tented to kill off the infestation. Our neighbors were delighted because tenting our house helped reduce termites in the neighborhood. We were told that the wood furniture in the house during the tenting would be protected from getting termites in the future.

house tenting for termites in Hawaii

When the humidity and pressure are just right, termites rise up from the ground in massive clouds and cover trees, houses, and everything. Termites can

77

also hitch a ride into a house on furniture or other wood products. A friend got an "amazing deal" on a luxurious leather chair at a garage sale, but while unloading it from his truck he set it down hard on the driveway and discovered it was infested with termites. Though garage sales may seem like a great way to furnish a house cheaply, in Hawaii used furniture may not be the best bargain.

B52 Cockroaches

"That's it I am out of here!" "I am never going to live any place that has bugs like that!" We have often heard people say this the first time they encountered one of Hawaii's gigantic flying cockroaches. People in Hawaii call them B52's after B52 bombers. Resorts and hotels go to great lengths to keep cockroaches under control so you rarely see them on their grounds, but these oversized bugs are common in Hawaii. The big, ugly ones are about 3 inches long and look more like a bird than a bug until they land and you can see that it is a giant cockroach. We have had several encounters with B52s that flew into our house through the open garage door. We were able to smash all but one with a shoe in under a minute. One managed to get away by getting under the stove. Fortunately, we had a new roach motel with sticky glue on the inside for just such an occasion. We put it in the kitchen and before we went to bed we looked in the "hotel" and found the giant cockroach had checked in, much to our comfort. Though they look scary, they are rarely a problem and window and door screens will keep them out.

Ten inch Centipedes

Centipedes are one of the few poisonous pests in Hawaii. Our first encounter with a big centipede in Hawaii was at a bed and breakfast. After watching the sunset from the hot tub, we walked back to our room in the twilight and came across a big centipede on the sidewalk. The owner stopped us before we got close saying, "stay back, they have a very painful sting". We watched as he skillfully cut the centipede into three parts with the edge of a dust pan. We were surprised to see that each piece was still "alive" and running around at top speed.

Our next encounter with a big centipede was at night in Hilo when we were lying in bed half asleep. We saw something snake-like squeeze through the not-so-tight fitting screen in the bedroom. It quickly darted under our bed. We turned on the light, got a shoe and for the next 20 minutes chased it around the bedroom smashing it with the shoe heel. Though no amount of shoe smashing killed it, we were eventually able to scoop it into a sealable plastic bag. We put the bag into the freezer and threw it in the trash right before the weekly pick up. In spite of centipedes being very hard to squish, we often found them dead on the lava rock perimeter around the house because they cannot survive dry heat and will die crossing just 30 inches of dry, hot rocks.

There are three species of centipedes in Hawaii, but only one has a dangerous bite. The poisonous centipede can grow to 10 inches in length and is long and flat with a brown head and dark green body with 21 body segments each with a pair of legs. They are most active at night and hide in shoes, clothing, under bedding, in cracks in the house, and under rocks, logs, leaves, and any dark, moist places. Bites can cause excruciating pain for several hours. A visit to a doctor or the local urgent care center may be required to deal with a bite and the pain.

Deafening Frogs and Cute Lizards

gecko on a honey bottle

Geckos

Geckos are everywhere in Hawaii. They come inside your living space at any opportunity, squeezing under screens and doors and zipping in when you open the door. We notice that some people seem to have strong reactions to them, either loving them or finding them disgusting and shrieking in dismay if they see one. We like them because they eat lots of bugs. They have big, cute eyes and vivid colors, but they get on any food left out, particularly anything sugary, and leave their droppings everywhere. The best way to keep geckos out is with tight fitting screens and making sure there are no gaps between doors and the floor or in window air conditioner units.

Coqui Frogs

Coqui frogs were accidentally introduced into Hawaii from Puerto Rico and they have flourished on Hawaii Island, Maui, and Oahu. Unlike Puerto Rico, the frogs in Hawaii do not have predators, so they grow larger and have mating calls that are much louder. Studies have found that the noise they make is loud enough to permanently damage your hearing. The area they inhabit in Hawaii is growing and they are spreading by hitching rides on cars, boats, and produce.

We lived for a month in a coqui frog infested area and the first week we thought the noise was cute. We were in a unit on the twelfth floor where you would think a little frog on the ground would not be a concern. The second week they seemed louder and by the end of the month the chorus of frogs started to really bother us. Some people have had to move because of the noise and sleep loss. A friend in Hilo hired someone to come every night to kill the frogs closest to her house, which allowed her to get some sleep most nights, although she was bitter about the $800 a month she had to pay for the professional "de-frogger".

When we lived in a house in Hilo, a neighbor did the "de-frogging". We never figured out who it was, but whenever we heard a coqui frog chirping at night, we would later hear, "whack, whack, whack", and then silence. We tried to be good neighbors and do some frog whacking ourselves. So when we heard frog chirping we put on a head lamp and went out to hunt. The frog chirps are high pitched, so it is not easy to determine the direction they are coming from. As soon as we got close to a chirping sound it would stop. In spite of many nights trying to locate a frog, we never found a single one. Clearly "de-frogging" is a job for the "professionals".

Areas with large coqui frog populations often have lower rents and lower property prices which is great if you are not sensitive to their noise. Coqui frogs only chirp at night and only above a certain temperature, so if you are trying to determine if an area has a coqui frog infestation, on a cool night or during pouring rain, you may not be able to tell that they are there.

Noisy Birds and Bothersome Rodents

Hawaii roosters

The Joys and Aggravation of Tropical Birds

Waking up to the sounds of tropical birds is one of the things we love about Hawaii. We have been entertained by the endless antics of myna birds that spent their winters around our house in Hilo. They jumped on the roof like it was a musical instrument and sat on the porch rail to glare at us through the window. We discovered that myna birds had pecked through a roof vent and had made a nest in the attic. Every spring several pairs of myna birds had long, protracted fights over which couple had the privilege of nesting there that year. Roof vents with heavy duty screens are the best way to keep birds and other pests from entering the house.

Roosters, peacocks, and other loud birds often wander around neighborhoods and their squawking can wake people up at night. Chickens run free in many communities and roost in tall trees making noise and covering the tree, ground, and cars parked in the shade with their droppings. Even in upscale residential areas and condominium complexes, loud roosters in the neighborhood crow every time a car headlight shines towards them. Oahu recently had a case where a woman was arrested for killing a peacock living in her residential community because it kept her up every night. Though she eventually won her case, many people have difficulty getting their neighbors to agree that their loud birds are a problem.

Mice, Rats, and red-eyed Rat things

Like most places, Hawaii has mice and rats, however they are a bigger concern in Hawaii because they can carry and spread dangerous tropical diseases. The last outbreak of the plague in Hawaii was in 1949 on the Hamakua coast of the island of Hawaii. Rodents in Hawaii commonly spread murine typhus, leptospirosis, and salmonellosis.

Hawaii has three types of rats. The biggest is the Norway rat which is black or brown in color and up to 10 inches long. The roof rat can be up to 7 inches long and loves to nest in banana and papaya trees and attics. The smallest and least seen is the Polynesian or Hawaii rat which is 5 inches long and tends to live away from houses. It is so small it looks more like a big mouse than a rat. The house mouse in Hawaii is smaller than the rats and is found in urban and rural areas.

Another rodent abundant in Hawaii is the mongoose, a long rat-like creature with red eyes and a tail. Mongoose are active during the day, so you see them a lot in Hawaii. The Indian mongoose was brought to Hawaii for the purpose of eating mice and rats in the sugar cane fields, but while the mice and rats are active at night, the mongoose are asleep. As a result, the mongoose eat everything else in sight including fruit, vegetables, birds, and wild eggs during the day. Their numbers are overwhelming, particularly on Maui and Hawaii, and since they have no natural predators, people use poison and traps to try and keep their numbers under control.

Mold and Acid Rain

green algae growing on the sidewalk

Mold, mildew, algae, and fungi are a constant battle in the moist, tropical climate of Hawaii. The volcanic fumes cause the rain to be highly acidic which is ideal for growing molds and fungi. Using air conditioners and dehumidifiers to control dampness is expensive because of the high cost of electricity. Most people try to keep the humidity down with fans and airflow. When it rains for weeks at a time, that approach does not work.

In Hilo, we used a small dehumidifier and tried every variety of moisture absorbing product. We used "Damp-Rid" products which consist of dried clay in a permeable bag that absorbs humidity creating a liquefied clay. Some versions allow you to reuse the clay by cooking it in the oven or plugging it into an electric socket to dry out. Both of those options require electricity. We use packets of dried clay in our closets, dressers, plastic containers with important photos and documents, and in our car. Long exposure to humidity destroys books, clothes, paintings, and most things.

After weeks of heavy rain, sidewalks and driveways are covered by thick, slippery, algae. To get rid of it we bought a pressure washer, but it did not just "wash off". It took the super high pressure tip and a lot of patience to blast the algae off. It was a huge task and increased our water bill by about $40 every time we did it. The algae grew back so quickly, it felt silly to do it.

Like most places near the ocean, salty ocean breezes rust metal and dissolve screens, wires, paint, and wood. Keeping rust at bay requires regular washing and replacing. On the island of Hawaii the acidic rain from the volcanic emissions (vog) adds to the destruction of metal, wood and building materials.

Chapter Eight
Hawaii's Residential Choices

Finding the Lifestyle you Want

ocean view in Waikiki

Hawaii offers a variety of neighborhood and lifestyle choices. You can live on a beach, in a high-rise, on an off-the-grid acreage, on a huge ranch, or in a tropical rainforest. Depending upon your financial situation and your personal tastes you can live in luxury or low cost housing, in a high-density area or on an acreage far from other people.

Once you have picked the climate you prefer, finding the residential lifestyle that matches your desires and needs is the next choice that can make your life in Hawaii more satisfying and fun.

- Do you want to be near a university, shopping malls, movie theaters, or restaurants?
- How close to the beach do you want to be, to snorkeling spots, or to a boat harbor?
- Do you prefer black lava or white sandy beaches?
- Do you want access to a swimming pool, bike path, hiking trails, or sports club?
- Do you want a garden or prefer to have someone else do grounds maintenance ?
- Do you prefer high-rises with a city view or single story dwellings with a garden view?
- Do you want to be close to town or off-the-grid in charge of your own utilities?

Knowing what you want will help to narrow your search to specific areas of the islands.

City Living in Hawaii

high-rise living along Ala Wai canal in Honolulu

If you are looking for city-living, Honolulu is really the only choice in Hawaii. It has the most shopping, night life, concerts, and the greatest concentration of jobs in the state of Hawaii. The administration of Honolulu is merged with the entire island of Oahu as the county of Honolulu with a single Mayor, council and budget. The incorporated area of the city of Honolulu stretches from Hawaii Kai to the Punchbowl and includes Waikiki, the Ala Wai canal, Manoa, the State Capital district, China town, Ala Moana, Diamond Head, Koko Head, Hanauma Bay, Aliamanu, and Salt Lake. The city's population is under 400,000, but the entire metro area of Honolulu is over 950,000 as of the 2010 census.

In addition to beaches, yacht harbors, and botanical parks, Honolulu has a zoo, aquarium, golf courses, museums, malls, universities, a great bus system, and an international airport. The prices tend to be high for homes and rentals in Honolulu because of the limited amount of space and the high demand. Most of the state's universities and trade schools are located in Honolulu including the University of Hawaii, Hawaii Pacific University, and Chaminade University bringing students to the city from around the state and world. The state and county governments, military bases, hospitals, malls, restaurants, hotels, and schools provide jobs and create a shortage of housing.

Being in the middle of the Pacific, the city draws people from the Philippines, Pacific Islands, Thailand, and South America hoping for a better life as well as wealthy people from America, Japan, and Asia looking for a second home. It is not unusual for students, young people, and families to pack into extremely small places to share the rent. The homeless are a constant challenge to the city. Most residents live in dense high-rise buildings and residential neighborhoods and face epic traffic jams on the few freeways that connect the highly populated areas of the city. Almost 20% of Hawaii's population is foreign born, the majority from the Philippines, China, and Japan. Many restaurants, clubs and businesses cater only to people from these countries, so if you are not fluent in that language they may not be able to serve you.

Waikiki has a year-round holiday feel with fireworks every Friday night, street performers, all night bars, clubs, and designer stores with more sales than Paris or Rome. Though it is focused on serving tourists, Waikiki has a large population of university students and residents living in the high-rise condominiums between the beach and the Ala Wai canal. This high density housing is close to jobs and schools and renowned for noise, traffic, and a problematic sewer system. Noise, prostitution, and public intoxication varies in Waikiki from block to block, but the great surfing, restaurants, and nearby jobs and entertainment make it the place to live for many people.

We moved to Waikiki thinking that it would be an exciting and fun place to live. We loved being able to walk to grocery stores, coffee shops, the beach, and take advantage of the hotel bars for sunset cocktails. After a month, the noise and traffic started to get tiresome. We grew tired of dodging aggressive drivers while crossing the street and the loud fireworks every Friday started to get on our nerves. The Ala Wai frequently smelled like sewage and the building had interruptions in elevator service which we found challenging living on the 22nd floor. We decided to forego the nightlife and shopping for Hawaii Island where we like having less traffic, fewer people, and usually less noise.

Honolulu has more online resources with statistics and news about crime, income opportunities, neighborhoods, real estate prices, rentals, and social issues than the other areas in Hawaii. We found however, that no amount of online research prepared us for the actual experience of living in Waikiki.

Conventional Suburban Living in Hawaii

suburban neighborhood in Hawaii

Hawaii has some suburban housing communities that "look" just like those on the mainland. They even have strip malls, box stores, and chain restaurants nearby. If you look out the windows of many of these houses, you might think that you were in Kansas. This type of conventional housing is really expensive in Hawaii and often sells for five to ten times more than it would on the mainland. Most of the extra cost is due to the high land prices; residential lots ready for house construction in Hawaii routinely cost substantially more than an entire house in many parts of the mainland. Additionally, the cost of construction is higher due to expensive labor costs and the cost of shipping materials in from the mainland. We have mentioned before, mainland-style house designs need to be inspected for proper building techniques and materials since their construction and materials are not the norm for Hawaii and in most cases are not the best designs for Hawaii's climate.

When you drive through one of the suburban type neighborhoods in Hawaii, it might appear to be just like neighborhoods on the mainland, but the reality of living there may be quite different. Asian and Pacific Islanders commonly live in large, extended families with grandparents through great grandchildren in a single house. Sharing a house spreads the mortgage or rent payments among many incomes and the elders provide free care for the children. Sometimes you can tell how many people are living in a house by the number of cars parked in front, though not always. Shoes are another sign since people in Hawaii leave their shoes outside. So if you see a mountain of shoes of different sizes on the step, there may be a large extended family living there.

The recent collapse in housing prices in Hawaii has created some empty suburban neighborhoods on outer islands. A young family recently moved into a residential enclave similar to the one they lived in on the mainland expecting their neighbors to be families with children. After moving in they discovered they were the only residents in the neighborhood under 70 years old and were surrounded by abandoned foreclosures and second homes of wealthy retirees. In Hawaii you cannot tell what is going on in a neighborhood by comparing its appearance to neighborhoods on the mainland.

Resort Living in Hawaii

resort condos with ocean view in Hawaii

Resort living on a tropical, white sand beach is the dream of many visitors to Hawaii. After vacationing in a hotel with an ocean view, warm pool, hot tub, near golf courses and restaurants, many people yearn for a part-time or full-time retirement resort lifestyle. The islands of Oahu, Maui, Hawaii and Kauai have condominium and residential communities on white sand beaches with tropical gardens and amenities that make resort living a reality for those who can afford it. Condo units are available in high-rises or spread over acreages with golf courses, private beach clubs, restaurants, and health spas. Single dwelling houses in gated communities with lush grounds and amenities are also available.

Resort communities vary in price from tens of millions to a few hundred thousand, depending on the island and the amenities. If being walking distance to the beach is not a big deal for you, condos and communities farther from the beach are often less expensive. In Waikiki, for example, condos within a few blocks of the beach are expensive for what you get, but condos that are too far for most tourists to walk can give you more value for the price. Size is a big factor in price too, so if you can squeeze into a smaller space there are more options at lower prices. In Hawaii there is great diversity in prices for resort style living and foreclosures are pushing the prices down.

One issue with resort style condos and communities is that part-time residents and renters constantly change the social scene. During the high season, the pools are crowded with noisy parties and people come and go at all times of the day and night. Resort areas near vacation spots, have the most loud parades and special events that last until late at night. Although condo management can make life more peaceful by enforcing rules and keeping residents quiet, the fees for security and maintenance can be more than the mortgage and, unlike a fixed rate mortgage, they can be raised at any time.

Small Town Living in Hawaii

Hilo Town

Outside of Honolulu, the majority of the residents of Hawaii live in small towns dotted throughout the islands. A town in Hawaii is more of a collection of residences than the concept of a town or city on the mainland since there are no incorporated areas outside of Honolulu. There is no way for a town in Hawaii to tax, float a bond, have special laws, or create boundaries. Residents rely on the county or the state for their police, fire protection, roads, schools, civil defense, hospital, water, garbage dumps, and all other services. Any infrastructure projects like new water wells or roads are complex and political since residents are competing with the rest of the state for funds and you cannot just jump in the car and drive to Honolulu to make your case. Road repairs, building permits, and most services can be hard to get in a small town when a single office is handling every request for the entire island.

Aside from the hotels and other tourist related jobs, Hawaii's largest employers in most towns are hospitals, schools, and the state and county governments. The high cost of energy and lack of natural resources makes Hawaii's secondary industries primarily low-tech like fishing, farming, ranching, food production, and services. Counties must share any taxes generated from hotel rooms and retail with the state to cover their expenses leaving less money available on the outer islands. The only guaranteed income that counties have is from property taxes.

The remoteness and lack of services and funding makes those who understand the state and county system and are able to get projects accomplished very desirable as friends and acquaintances. We have come to prize the knowledge and skills of people who know how to resolve problems and make things happen in Hawaii. We have met retired military men who seem to know everything about how to make mechanical things work and survive off the grid and elderly Japanese ladies who are adept at getting through county red-tape to get projects accomplished. In Hawaii it is most often through relationships and family that projects, like a community well or road, get funded and completed.

<u>Remote Residential Acreages in Hawaii</u>

country road in Hawaii

Residential acreages are common on the islands of Maui and Hawaii where there is more land and substantially less people than Oahu. The district of Puna on the southeast corner of the island of Hawaii, is larger than the entire island of Oahu and has numerous subdivisions with residential lots for sale. Hawaiian Paradise Park (HPP), alone has over 8800 lots which when combined with the many other subdivisions along Highway 30, has made Puna the fastest growing population in Hawaii. The district of Kau on the island of Hawaii also has numerous residential subdivisions like the Hawaii Ocean View Estates (HOVE) subdivision near South Point which has 10,697 one acre lots. These remote acreages are usually in Agricultural districts and can be used for residences, farms, or ranches. Within the same subdivisions, acreages can range from lush tropical forests to barren lava fields.

Since remote acreages are often available at "reasonable" prices, some people buy lots sight unseen just to have their acre of paradise. They later discover the downside of remote property in Hawaii. Basic utilities like electric, water, cell service, and cable are limited or completely unavailable in many remote areas. Insurance can be difficult if not impossible to get if the property is in a flood zone, lava zone, or outside of fire station coverage. The point of entry into some remote subdivisions is a single road, making a quick evacuation due to a fire or other disasters impossible. With county services stretched thin on many of the islands, you are on your own when dealing with the weather, thieves, wild pigs, and any other hazards.

We have a friend who loved living in the town of Hilo but thought his $800 a month rent was too high. He had a rural property in Puna and calculated that he could build a place on it and live there for far less than the cost of his rent. Ten years later he was spending $800 a month just on gas and he had to replace his cars often as the bad roads wore out the shocks, steering, and tires. Driving distances that seem short on a map may take a long time because of slow trucks, road construction, rainy weather, and the poor condition of the road. He was considering moving back to town just to save on his gas and vehicle expenses.

The low cost of land in some areas of Hawaii can give the illusion of cheap housing, but when factoring in all the costs of living remotely, it may be more expensive than living in a town.

One of the challenges is obtaining water in remote areas without water service. Water catchment systems are the standard for remote residential properties and it is estimated that up to 60,000 people in the state, mostly on the island of Hawaii, are dependent on them to capture rainwater for their water supply. These systems require proper maintenance and water treatment to provide water that is free of contamination. Though rainwater can be used for bathing, washing, flushing, laundry, and gardening it cannot safely be used as drinking water. The acidic rain in Hawaii due to the volcanic emissions, combined with salty sea air causes the catchment systems to rust and mold.

Remote residential property usually allows you to grow your own food, have livestock, and live without utility bills. In a tropical rain forest even a small acreage can sustain a few cattle and papayas and other locally grown food can supplement grass fed livestock. For many people, their fantasy of having a tropical farm or grazing horses on the grassy slopes of a volcano are realized in Hawaii. We admire the plucky families that live off-the-grid using solar power, collecting rain water, and driving on sub-par roads. They live without cable or internet access. We have however, met many couples that bought remote acreages in Puna or along the Hamakua Coast not realizing the amount of labor required to haul in drinking water and food and maintain the property. After a few years, they regretted choosing a place so far from activities, shopping, entertainment and social gatherings.

Several decades ago, we lived on a remote acreage on the mainland. We grew tired of the long drive to a grocery store, friends, and activities. We quickly found out that we did not have the skills needed to fulfill our great plan to grow our own food and learned that we missed living near shopping, entertainment, and an airport. In spite of our experience, we currently own remote acreage on Hawaii Island and fantasize about living there one day. So far, we are finding living in a gated condo, across from a white sand beach in Kona, more appealing.

cows on a ranch in Hawaii

Chapter Nine
Hawaii's Complex Property Zoning

Property Zoning can Spoil a Dream Home

parcel blocked entry by Hawaii Law

Property zoning in Hawaii is dictated by a complex web of historic laws and current state laws and managed by numerous organizations including the State Land Use Commission, the State Board of Land and Natural Resources, Hawaii Homelands, and individual county planning commissions. The development and use of property is controlled by its zoning district, size, historic Kuleana rights, grandfather clauses, and permits. The reality is that in Hawaii no property title is entirely free of encumbrances because of the nature of the land division and historic claims to land that are still in effect, as well as Hawaii State's claim to all property mineral rights.

When people buy real estate in Hawaii they often make assumptions about what a neighborhood will and will not allow. If a lot is in a gated community with nice homes they assume that a pig farm cannot move in next door. In order to combat the wide spread conversion of agricultural zoned land to gated enclaves of second homes for non-residents, the Hawaii State Legislature passed a law making it hard, if not impossible, for members of a home owners community built on Agricultural zoned land to sue for breach of the owners covenants. It can cause a lot of frustration and grief to suddenly discover that you cannot stop someone from building a horse barn or chicken farm next to your dream house.

Whether you are buying a house, acreage, or a condo, it is worth researching the property's zoning, permits, titles, and association rules. Sellers and realtors are often vague about the details of the property and some counties are very relaxed in their enforcement. The details of property land records and its zoning and codes are available from the Bureau of Conveyances in Honolulu. Finding out that your property is not what you thought it was after the purchase can jeopardize your plans for a happy Hawaii home.

Kuleana and Native Hawaiian Property Rights

In the 1840s the King of Hawaii instigated property zoning so that it was more like the westernized system with land titles. Hawaii lands were divided up among the Kingdom, Chiefs, and the Territorial government. In 1850, a law was passed allowing native tenants to claim title to the lands they worked and acquire what is known as a Kuleana parcel. Today Kuleana rights are still attached to the land irrespective of the owners of the title or deed. The rights attached to the decedents of the original Kuleana owners include: access, agricultural use, gathering and religious ceremony rights, rights to a single-family dwelling, water rights, and fishing rights. Kuleana rights extend to an adjoining property if it is the only way to gain access to a nearby Kuleana and even the rights to water in a stream. Many of the Kuleana are never used, but at any time a group or individual could show up and plant taro or construct a house on a Kuleana parcel within the property you own.

Even if a property does not have a Kuleana, native Hawaiians may still have the right to gather on it for religious or cultural purposes. The Hawaii Supreme Court ruled that Hawaii Revised Statutes section 7-1 protected the gathering rights of native Hawaiians on Molokai on private property. The Pele Defense Fund won a case that gave them access to private land for religious purposes based on the land's historic use. In another case, a building permit issued by Hawaii County to develop a resort was successfully challenged when the Hawaii Supreme Court ruled that native Hawaiians retained rights to pursue traditional and customary activities on the property. The Hawaii

Supreme Court did clarify that "fully developed" residential property is not open to native Hawaiian gathering rights.

Establishment of State Property Districts

Another change to property zoning in Hawaii occurred in 1961 when the Hawaii State Legislature adopted the State Land Use Law (Chapter 205, Hawaii Revised Statutes) which classified all the land in the state into one of four zoning districts: Conservation, Agricultural, Rural and Urban. The purpose of the new law was partially to keep land from being used inappropriately by developers that were converting prime agricultural land to residential use and scattering housing developments across the islands which stretched public services. The Legislature established the State Land Use Commission (LUC) to administer the law. The LUC established the district boundaries for the entire state and hears petitions for boundary changes submitted by private landowners, developers and state and county agencies. The commission also acts on requests for special use permits within the Agricultural and Rural districts. The law was amended in 1985 to allow applicants for land use changes of 15 acres or less to apply to the county where the property is located. The commission only handles requests for property less than 5 acres when they are in the Conservation district.

Conservation District

Property in the Conservation district is solely under state jurisdiction and not controlled at the county level. It is divided into four main subzones: Protective, Limited, Resource, and General, with Protective being the most strict and General being the least strict. There is also a "Special" subzone that can accommodate unique projects. If Conservation district land is designated as a Special Management Area (SMA) for things like alternate energy production, then the county is given some input into the use.

The State Land Use Commission controls the boundaries and classification of Conservation district zoning. However, the Department of Land and Natural Resources (DLNR) has administrative responsibility over the Conservation district land. The limited range of uses of property in the Conservation district usually requires a Conservation District Use Permit (CDUP) which is issued by the State Board of Land and Natural Resources (BLNR). The BLNR can approve single-family homes in the Resource and General subzones, and in some situations, in the Limited subzone. The BLNR can also approve, through a CDUP, such things as highways, infrastructure for utilities, and resource-dependent power plants such as hydro or geothermal power.

Although this may seem like a rare land classification, almost 50% or 1,973,631 acres of the total land in Hawaii (4,112,388 acres) is classified as Conservation district land.

Urban Districts

Since Hawaii has no incorporated municipalities or cities, except for Honolulu, Urban district zoning is really just a property designation by some counties with a concentration of people, structures, and services. Jurisdiction of Urban district property lies with the respective counties and lot sizes and permitted uses are established by county ordinances, codes, and rules.

Rural Districts

Rural districts are usually composed of small farms mixed with low-density residential lots with a minimum size of one-half acre. Jurisdiction over Rural districts is shared by the State Land Use Commission and county governments. Permitted uses include those relating or compatible to agricultural use and low-density residential lots. Variances can be obtained through the special use permitting process.

Agricultural Districts

Agricultural districts are administered by each county within the framework of the state land use law. Hawaii State law and the State Land Use Commission rules limit the use of land in the Agricultural district, most of them relating to agriculture including the cultivation of crops, aquaculture, raising livestock, wind energy facilities, timber cultivation, agriculture-support activities and land with significant potential for agriculture uses. Uses permitted in the highest productivity agricultural categories (A and B) are governed by statute. Uses in the lower-productivity categories (C, D, E or U) are established by the

Commission and include those allowed on A or B lands as well as those stated under Section 205-4.5, Hawaii Revised Statutes.

Lot sizes for subdivisions in the Agricultural district are set by the county council through zoning, but must be at least one acre by state law. Lots within subdivisions that were approved before June 4, 1976 have different rules than lots in subdivisions approved after that date. Homes in subdivisions approved after June 4, 1976 must be "farm dwellings", or at least related to agriculture, but any subdivisions approved before that date can have "single family dwellings". Each county taxes Agricultural districts differently, some relying on the zoning and others appraising the land to verify that it is actually being used as a farm.

A "special permit" can be issued for any "unusual and reasonable" use. For areas of 15 acres or less, the county planning commissions get to decide the special permit, but for properties larger than 15 acres, the special permit must be approved by both the county and the State Land Use Commission. Examples of common special permits are bed-and-breakfast operations and cell phone towers.

Almost 50% of the land in Hawaii is in the Agricultural district zone (1,930,224 acres) which includes land with a high potential for agricultural use as well as bone-dry lava fields with very low potential for productive agricultural activity.

Looking at the structures built on the property or next to a property does not tell you much about the zoning. Builders are notorious for putting upscale houses on property in Agricultural districts. You may buy a new house in an area that appears to be all residential but find that there is no legal way to stop a family pig farm from moving in next door. In Hawaii County, for example, the majority of the remote residential acreages in gated communities are in Agricultural districts allowing a neighbor to attain a permit for a wind farm or bio-fuel plant.

It is a risky and complex proposition to depend on getting the state or county planning commissions to change the zoning district of the property or provide a variance to build a structure or use the property in a way that is not allowed.

House and Structure Permits

Hawaii has unpermitted structures and portions of structures, particularly in remote areas. Just because a house is built there does not mean that it is permitted or built based on the permit issued by the county. You can choose to ignore the lack of permits for a house, cesspool, swimming pool, porch, garage or other structure, but doing so means you take the risk that structures may have to be removed at your expense later on. You may also be assessed fines if the county later decides to enforce their building permits.

You can find out what the county records claim about the property by looking at the online tax office property records available by each county in the state. These records may not contain all the information that the county has, but will give you some information about the property. You can search for properties by address or parcel number. The parcel number, or Tax Map Key (TMK), searches give better results. A TMK number is a unique number assigned by the county for each parcel of land, lot, or condo. The 6 part number includes information about which island it is on as well as its county assigned TMK Zone (not to be confused with the property zoning), section, plat, parcel and CPR or condominium number. MLS records in Hawaii almost always provide the TMK number with the listing.

The online county parcel or TMK records provide the owner's name and address. If the property is leasehold, which is common for condominiums and commercial properties in Hawaii, then the owner leasing the land will show up as one of the owners of the property. The online data also has information about previous sales of the property, permits issued, property size, zoning of the property, details of any residential or commercial buildings, a sketch of the structure and property, the valuation of the land and structures for tax purposes, current and previous tax bills, and maps of the property's location. The information shown is sometimes incomplete, but it is worth investigating to see if the ownership or major structures are different from what you are expecting.

Conditions, Covenants and Restrictions

Many residential communities have conditions, covenants, and restrictions (CC&Rs) on the buildings and use of the property. The CC&Rs are normally provided as a part of the real estate sale and the sale is often contingent on the new owners signing them. In Hawaii, CC&R's can be complicated by a change in status of the real estate, for example, if it was once leasehold and later converted to fee simple. The CC&Rs created by the original leaseholder may still be in effect even though the leaseholder is no longer involved in the property in any way. Some people choose to ignore the historic CC&Rs assuming that they will not be enforced, but that is a potential risk. On the other hand, some residential communities have created CC&Rs that conflict with the state law usage for the land. For example, land in an Agriculture district, converted to 3 acre homesteads cannot prohibit agricultural use of the land with CC&Rs. Therefore CC&Rs created by an organization like a homeowners or road maintenance association may not protect a land owner from a neighbor using their acreage for agricultural use.

Condo Owner Rules

In addition to zoning laws, housing and condo complexes usually have their own strict rules and regulations. Condo units may be allowed to have short term rentals or they may be restricted to rentals of only 30 days or more. If you are counting on an income from a short term rental program, make sure

110

it is allowed before you buy. If you are planning on quiet days around the pool, make sure the complex is not being run like a hotel with a new party showing up each day. Condos have rules about animals, parking, plants, noise, BBQ's, and more. Our condo in Kona, for example, has a thick handbook of rules and regulations with fairly major things like no dogs. As a part of buying a condo, the owners association usually requires the buyer to sign that they read and understand all the rules. This allows the association to levy fines for every violation and put a lien against the property for rule infractions, missing payments, and late fees. The strictness with which the rules are enforced are highly dependent on the owners association, the current board of directors, and the manager of the complex.

Property Metes and Bounds

Real estate sales often do not require a new survey and instead rely on old documents or claims by the seller. We always pay for our own survey as a part of any property purchase and in every case we have been surprised about where the property lines were located. In one case, the survey put water catchment tanks for a mountain cabin in the middle of the road on the plat the land developers provided to the county. The road crew for the developer misunderstood the survey pins and put the road over the lots. In another case, a survey showed that a house we were planning to buy had a car port on the property line. Knowing this in advance allowed us to include a requirement for the seller to get his neighbor to give his permission for a variance regarding the car port location in order to close the deal.

property boundary marked in Hawaii

Trying to guess where property lines are located can be risky since lava fields, steep terrain, and vegetation can make it hard to walk the lines. Another benefit of a surveyor is they may be able to tell you about any lava tubes or animals living on the property. One surveyor we spoke to said he marvels that people will build a $200,000 house without spending $400 to make sure it is built on the land they bought.

Property Deeds and Titles

We have found title insurance a good investment to insure we own the property free and clear, or at least to get our money back if we do not. Title insurance companies verify that the sellers are the only names on the title and there are no other liens. More and more property sales, like foreclosures and short sales, are taking place without any verification that the title of the property is clear. Even if it is clear, getting title insurance can insure that nothing goes wrong later.

Following one of our purchases of a property on the island of Hawaii, the county discovered a box of old titles that had not been included during their switch from paper to electronic land records. Rather than verifying whether newer transactions had occurred on each property, they updated existing property records with the owners registered in the old records. As a result, our property suddenly showed three additional owners from land records over 30 years old. Our title insurance company was saddled with the expense of hiring a lawyer to track down the "owners", or their descendants, on the mainland to get signatures that released their "claim" to the property. It took over two years. During that time, we did not have clear title to sell the property, however, the title insurance company was prepared to buy the land at our purchase price. The money we saved on that one policy has more than covered the cost of all of our title policies in the past.

Chapter Ten
Hawaii's Unique Culture

Life in the Slow Lane

The adage that says "Hawaii either embraces you or spits you out" is based on the problems so many newcomers have dealing with Hawaii's uniquely different culture. Those that can adjust to the slower pace and get along with their neighbors will find the greatest acceptance and peace.

Polynesian cultures have a different view of ownership, family, money, and operate at a different pace than the mainland and most big cities in the world. In Hawaii, spear fishing and surfing are considered work and "talking story" to a customer is more important than serving the long line of people waiting to check out at the grocery store counter. Some find Hawaii's politics, laid-back workers, and food stamp lifestyle too frustrating to live with.

We have found that being open to the cultural differences and slowing down in our expectations of what we can accomplish makes living in Hawaii more fun. When we first arrived we were frustrated by how slow people drive on Hawaii Island. Drivers are often so busy talking and waving their hands they cannot drive very fast, but now we find ourselves driving slowly and wondering why rental cars behind us keep weaving around looking for a chance to pass. Over time, the pace and culture have come to seem normal.

Another difference in Hawaii, particularly on the less populated islands, is the approach to disputes. We have learned that calling in the "authorities" rarely solves a problem and police and school administrators often leave it to neighbors and parents to keep the peace. We have had to deal with a neighborhood problem by going door to door to get support to pressure a neighbor into changing the situation.

Acting like you have authority, being impatient or pushy will usually result in the opposite of what you want to happen. Much of what ranks on the mainland like your income, position, resume, and accomplishments have little value on the islands. Being happy in Hawaii is a balance of living in the appropriate neighborhood for your lifestyle combined with being able to appreciate or at least keep from being frustrated with the differences in culture.

Racism and Culture in Hawaii

Hawaii's population is a mix of Asians, Polynesians, Portuguese, Filipinos, Caucasians, and Hispanics. Though we work and live together, each group has a strong identity and close family and cultural ties. Most of the residents in Hawaii live in relative peace and harmony in their neighborhoods, attending the same schools and participating together in community and cultural events. However, some of the neighborhoods are predominately one race or another and it may take a while before neighbors warm up to newcomers, or they may never.

In some Asian cultures it is not common to be "friendly" with neighbors. In some neighborhoods, the lots were partitioned by a family for each of their children to have their own house. When you move in you may feel like everyone is being friendly to everyone except you and in fact they may all be related. Residents are sometimes slow to welcome newcomers to their neighborhoods and social groups because of the constant flow of mainlanders that move to the islands and leave within a short time. While living in Hilo, we met dozens of new retirees that moved to the area from the mainland, bought a house, and fully furnished it. Our friends would laugh that they would be buying their new beds and furniture at a garage sale within a year, and in most cases they were right.

Though racism has a negative connotation in America, in Hawaii it is deeply ingrained in the culture and even the state's laws. People are highly aware of their racial makeup and race is called out in song and dance. Hawaiian words for each race (haole, popolo, kanaka, kepani, pilpino, pake, kolea, kamoa, sepania, pukiki) are used in conversation, local songs, and hapa-hula. Hapa (half) Hawaiian songs are regularly performed in schools, at festivals, and in bars. The combination of racial awareness, family size, and small town familiarity can result in newcomers feeling discriminated against when they are ignored at a restaurant or business or treated differently by county workers and police.

Some claim there is no racism because there is no majority race in the islands where about 38% of the population are Asians (including Japanese, Filipino, Chinese and Koreans), 27% are Caucasians, 9% are Hawaiian or Polynesians and over 22% are two or more races. However, these percentages vary considerably from town to town and neighborhood to neighborhood within Hawaii. Haole (which means "one without breath" in Hawaiian) refers to white people or Caucasians. Active and vocal separatist groups wanting independence for Hawaiians from the US have created anti-Caucasian sentiments in some communities.

Hawaiian language charter schools, funded by the state, center their learning around the Polynesian way of life and some perpetuate negative feelings about being part of the US and the mistreatment of Hawaiians. Some newcomers from the American continent find being a minority an unexpected and uncomfortable change.

sign during Hawaii 50th anniversary of statehood

We have been frustrated by some local businesses that wait on white people last or not at all. We have made peace with this by not spending money at these businesses and by acknowledging that Hawaiians still endure significant racism from white people. In one case we were completely mortified as a highly educated newcomer to Hawaii ranted at a public meeting that no Hawaiian was able to get a PhD in his field, though one of his new colleagues was Hawaiian with a PhD in his field. He did not last two years in his job. When we find ourselves gasping at the racist things we hear white people say in social settings, it reminds us to ignore the racism we get. We realize, however, that dealing with racist co-workers or teachers in your children's school may not be easy or advisable to ignore.

We have had some experiences of racism in Hawaii that made us realize that the discrimination and the local resident's frustration with whites is often deeper than skin color. While living in Hilo, we were warmly accepted into several social circles with people of Japanese, Filipino and Polynesian decent. It was wonderful, because being raised in Asia, we had missed the types of relationships and interactions we had growing up. Our son was on an exchange in Japan at the time and we were given helpful advice about how to navigate some complex cultural issues we were having with his host family. A year later, when our son returned to Hilo we introduced him to our friends. They all stared at his pale, white skin and blue eyes in shock stammering, "He's... well he's ... he's white!". We realized then that we had been passing as "brown by behavior". Though sometimes people react only to your skin color, often people in Hawaii are reacting to your "cultural behaviors".

Staying in a resort hotel does not prepare you for living in the culture of Hawaii because workers are paid to smile, ignore rude behaviors, and be "aloha". Being a minority can subject your family to a very different social situation in Hawaii than what you have ever experienced on the mainland. We have met young couples shocked to discover on the first day of school that their child was the only Caucasian in the classroom. We have also met many mixed race families that found Hawaii a haven, where for the first time they and their children felt at home, treated with respect, and in harmony with the mixed races in the community. Towns, neighborhoods, businesses, and schools vary widely in their racial makeup which changes the shopping, schooling, and living experience substantially.

Importance of Good Neighbors

Living on an island you quickly find out how dependent you are on each other, particularly on the less populated islands in Hawaii. In any catastrophe, you have only your neighbors to dig you out of a collapsed house or take you to the hospital. Food, water, and assistance may be weeks away after a tsunami or hurricane and county and hospital personnel are in short supply. We discovered that being a good neighbor is a key part of creating friendly neighbors. Without a doubt the biggest problem we have had in Hawaii is living next to awful neighbors. Finding a home in a neighborhood where you can keep "the aloha" can make the difference between happiness or misery in Hawaii.

After moving into our house in Hilo, we realized that there was a big difference between having the windows wide open all the time and the tightly closed, double-pane thermal windows we had in northern California. We could hear and smell everything in the neighborhood from the coffee grinder and alarm clocks in the morning to the phone calls and drunken parties at night. Losing sleep at night from rowdy neighbors, dogs, bars, and loud events is the major complaint of newcomers to Hawaii.

After we lived a year in a quiet Hilo neighborhood, an elderly neighbor sold her house to a local investor who planned to get an income stream from rent. To get the most income, the investor rented to six college students from the mainland. Once they moved in we had a loud party next door almost every night. Although we were only two blocks from the police station, the police refused to take action in spite of the nightly calls from us and our neighbors. We were ultimately able to address the problem by helping to organize the neighbors to pressure the investor and her family to evict the renters. When she was finally "convinced" to investigate, she discovered the original lease signers had left the state months earlier and to her dismay found major structural damage to the property from the dozens of drunk coeds that jumped up and down on the roof during parties.

We have had similar problems in Kona where some condo owners try to maximize their income by renting to large groups of loud, partying renters. Fortunately, we live in a complex with an active homeowners association and an excellent manager that is willing to fine owners that break the condo rules, which includes noise volume. Home owners associations are one way to deal with the lack of police intervention in Hawaii and they are taking on more security functions as counties in Hawaii cut back on the police force as tax income falls. We consider the neighbor factor so significant we are now leery even of renting without spending time to research the neighborhood.

How to Research an Area

Most people that move to Hawaii have been visiting the state for years. Many have family living in Hawaii or they return to the same town year after year for long vacations. They are best positioned for a move because they already know people, have joined churches and social groups, and have experienced some of the challenges of living in Hawaii. If you move to Hawaii after one or two short vacations, plan on spending a year or two figuring out how to live and make friends.

Our advice is to spend the time researching the lifestyle in Hawaii before moving and certainly before buying. We visited every island and spent at least a month on Maui, Oahu, and the island of Hawaii before deciding that Hawaii Island was for us. Some people may think that is excessive, but moving two cars and a container of belongings is a big investment and we thought it was worth the time to make sure it made sense. Researching a place should include a visit, talking to people, and imagining your new life there.

Visit the Place
Once you think you have identified an area in Hawaii of interest, take a long trip there. Go to the grocery stores, check the prices, and verify the availability of your favorite foods. Visit the post office, library, coffee houses, and businesses you may frequent or service organizations you will need when you live there. Visit

the hospital, check out the drug stores and verify that your medical insurance will be accepted by local doctors. If you need certain prescriptions or treatments, find out if they are available before you move. If you have children, visit the schools in advance and meet the teachers. Park in the neighborhoods you are interested in at night to hear the noise and observe the activity. Notice what people wear, what cars they drive, how they act, and especially how they treat you.

Talk to People

Just seeing a place is not enough, you really need to talk to people. The "coconut wireless" in Hawaii is the verbal exchange of information that in many cases is the only way to find out what is going on in an island community. People in Hawaii love to talk and are only too happy to "talk story" if you take the time and are willing to listen. You can find people at the public pools, parks, community centers, on the beach, and all sorts of places outside. People will tell you about the latest crimes, pest invasions, shark attacks, the best local places to buy produce, and what is going on in politics. If you are thinking about a condo, talk to the manager and anyone on the board to get a feel for what is going on in the complex and how friendly the environment will be. Talk to local insurance agents about the crime rates, fires, and hazards in the community.

Visualize your Life

Once you have visited the place, talked to people, and have a sense of what it might be like to live in a community, take the time to imagine your life there. Think about what your day will look like, what you will do in the mornings and evenings, and how your new life will achieve your dream life in Hawaii. Write it up and be sure to read it often after you move. It is said that "on an island you have only what you bring with you", so make sure to bring the right stuff and a written vision of your new, wonderful life in Hawaii so you can remember to live it every day once you get here.

Glossary

ahupua'a—land division usually extending from the slopes of the Volcano to the sea designated by a heap (ahu) of rocks

'aina—land, earth

aloha – greeting, goodbye, love "keep the aloha"

ha'ole—white person, person of Caucasian descent

hapa—part, fraction, mixed-race, part Hawaiian

hapa-haole or hapa-hula—Hawaiian songs or hula danced to songs (meles) in English

kama'aina—native born, now means resident of the state

Kamoa—Samoan

Kanaka—Polynesian, Native Hawaiian

Ka'u—District in Hawaii County

kapu—taboo, prohibited, sacred

Kepani—Japanese or Japanese descent

Kolea—Korean or Korean descent

Kona—district in Hawaii County, leeward, winds from the southwest

kuleana—right, privilege, responsibility, authority, business, property, estate, portion, jurisdiction, authority, interest, claim, small piece of property

lanai—veranda or covered porch

Lana'i—island in Hawaii

local—person born and raised in Hawaii

mahele—portion, division, section, zone, lot, piece, land division of 1848 (the Great Mahele)

mainland— the continental United States

makai—on the seaside, toward the sea (kai)

malama—to take care of, tend, attend, care for, preserve, protect

mauka—inland, upland, towards the volcano

'ohana – family, standalone unit on a property for family or friends to visit

outer islands—all the islands other than Oahu

Pake—Chinese descent

pali – cliff, steep hill

Pilpino—Filipino descent

Popolo—African, black person

Pukiki—Portuguese descent

Puna—district in Hawaii County, spring (water)

pu'u – hill, mount, lava cone

Sepania—Spanish, Latino descent

TMK—Tax Map Key, unique identifier for every property in Hawaii

tsunami—tidal wave

typhoon—hurricane or tropical cyclone

vog—volcanic emissions

Chapter References

Chapter One: A Hawaii-Style House

Canadian Wood Council, *Termite Control and Wood-Frame Buildings, Nov 2001,* Also at http://www.cwc.ca

HRS0196-6.5 Solar water heater law in Hawaii, Hawaii Revised Statutes, Also at http://www.capitol.hawaii.gov/hrscurrent/Vol03_Ch0121-0200D/HRS0196/HRS_0196-0006_0005.htm

Hwang, Dennis J. and Darren K. Okimoto, *Homeowner's Handbook to prepare for Natural Hazards*, University of Hawaii Sea Grant College Program, June 2007

Louisiana State University Agriculture Center, *Wind-resistant Roof design*, P Skinner & C Reichel, April 2010, Also at http://text.lsuagcenter.com/en/family_home/home/design_construction/Safer+Stronger+Smarter/Durability+Hazards/Flood+Wind+Water/Roof+Overhangs+and+Attachments.htm

Rither, Christopher, *Inspector Guide Series: Common Problems in Hawaii's Home*, Also at http://www.islandinspections.com/examplecommonproblemsbook.pdf

University of Hawaii, Department of Civil and Environmental Engineering, *Structural Seismic Retrofits for Hawaii Single-Family Residences with Post and Pier Foundations*, FEMA Hazard Mitigation Grant Program DR-1664-HI, May 2009

University of Hawaii at Manoa, Termite Project, *Homeowners Guide*, 2004, Also at http://www2.hawaii.edu/~entomol/guide

Chapter Two: A Hawaii Designed Garden

Ballantyne, Coco, "Watch out Hawaii: Veggies may harbor rare parasite", *Scientific American,* Jan 8, 2009, Also at http://www.scientificamerican.com/blog/post.cfm?id=watch-out-hawaii-veggies-may-harbor-2009-01-08

Ebesu, Richard, Integrated Pest Management for Home Gardens: Insect Identification and Control, Department of Plant and Environmental Protection Sciences, University of Hawaii at Manoa, July 2003, Also at http://www.ctahr.hawaii.edu/oc/freepubs/pdf/IP-13.pdf

Hawaiian Ecosystems at Risk Project (HEAR), *Invasive species information for Hawaii and the Pacific*, May 1997, Also at http://www.hear.org

Hollyer, JR et. al, *Best Food-Safety Practices for Hawai'i Gardeners* University of Hawaii, College of Tropical Agriculture and Human Resources, March 2011, Also at http://www.ctahr.hawaii.edu/oc/freepubs/pdf/FST-41.pdf
State of Hawaii Department of Health, *Fight the Bite*, November 2006, Also at

http://hawaii.gov/health/family-child-health/contagious-disease/wnv/pdf/brochure_mod.pdf

University of Hawaii at Manoa, College of Tropical Agriculture and Human Resources, *Publications on Hawaii plant diseases,* Also at http://www.ctahr.hawaii.edu/Site/PubList.aspx?key=Plant%20Disease

USDA, *Albizia, The tree that ate Puna*, Comfort Sumida, Flint Huges, Kathleen Friday, November 2005

Chapter Three: Buying or Building in Hawaii

HPM Building Supply, *Lauhala house kit design*, June 2011, Also at http://www.hpmhawaii.com

Hwang, Dennis J. and Darren K. Okimoto, *Homeowner's Handbook to prepare for Natural Hazards*, University of Hawaii Sea Grant College Program, June 2007

Rither, Christopher, *Inspector Guide Series: Common Problems in Hawaii's Home*, Book 2, Also at http://www.islandinspections.com/examplecommonproblemsbook.pdf

Wood Truss Council of America and Structural Building Component Association, *Framing the American Dream*, March 2009, Also at http://www.sbcindustry.com/images/publication_images/fad.pdf

Chapter Four: Costs of Home Ownership

City and County of Honolulu Department of Real Property Assessment Division, *Real Property Tax Rates in Hawaii Fiscal Year July 1, 2010 to June 20, 2011,* Also at http://www.realpropertyhonolulu.com/content/rpadcm s/documents/2010/10_rates.pdf;jsessionid=D821299 8048F1897F8AB46AD08C7525B

Hawaii Electric Company, Residential Services Electric Rates, Also at http://www.heco.com

State of Hawaii, Department of Commerce and Consumer Affairs, Homeowners Insurance Information, 2009, Also at http://hawaii.gov/dcca/ins/consumer/consumer_inf ormation/homeowners

Chapter Five: Hawaii's Unique Geography

Altonn, Helen "UH scientists to examine Kilauea undersea landslide", *Star-Bulletin,* December 1997, Also at http://archives.starbulletin.com/97/12/29/news/story 6.html

Businger, Steven, *Hurricanes in Hawaii*, poster for Hurricanes and Extreme Weather Phenomena Symposium presented by the Center for the Study of Active Volcanoes sponsored by FEMA, September 1998, Also at http://www.soest.hawaii.edu/met/Faculty/businger/po ster/hurricane/

FEMA, *Flood insurance study, Kauai County Hawaii,*
November 2010, Also at
http://www.hidlnr.org/eng/nfip/pdf/fis/Kauai%20Coun
ty/150002V001C.pdf

Hawaii Department of Land and Natural Resources,
Division of Forestry and Wildlife, *State of Hawai'i
Forest Reserve System,* Also at
http://www.state.hi.us/dlnr/dofaw/frs/page8.htm

Hawaii Department of Land and Natural Resources,
Division of State Parks, *Hawaii State Parks,* Also at
http://www.hawaiistateparks.org

Moore, J. G. et al, "Prodigious submarine landslides on
the Hawaiian Ridge", *Journal of Geophysical Research,*
Series B 12, Volume 94, No B12, pages 17,465-
17,484, December 1989

State of Hawaii, Important Information about VOG,
2011, Also at http://hawaii.gov/gov/vog

US GSA Office of Governmentwide Policy, *Federal Real
Property Profile,* online report, September 2004, p 19,
Also at
http://www.gsa.gov/graphics/ogp/Annual_Report__FY
2004_Final_R2M-n11_0Z5RDZ-i34K-pR.pdf

Chapter Six: Hawaii's Varied Climate Zones

Conservation Biology in Hawai'i, Ed. Charles and
Danielle Stone, "Chapter 13: Vegetation Zones of the
Hawaiian Islands", author Linda Cuddihy, University of
Hawaii Press, 1988, Also at
http://manoa.hawaii.edu/hpicesu/book/1988_chap/13
.pdf

Gavenda, Robert, "Hawaiian Quaternary Paleoenvironments: A Review of Geological, Pedagogical, and Botanical Evidence", *Pacific Science* (1992), vol. 46, no. 3: 295-307, Also at http://scholarspace.manoa.hawaii.edu/bitstream/hand le/10125/1409/v46n3-295-307.pdf

Hawaii Drought Monitor: Commission on Water Resource Management, El Nino, State of Hawaii, 1997, Also at http://hawaii.gov/dlnr/drought/forecast.htm

Juvik, James, et al, *Climate and Water Balance on the Island of Hawaii*, NOAA Mauna Loa Observatory Lab 20th Anniversary Report, pp 129-139, 1978

Leopold, Luna and CK Stidd, "A Review of Concepts in Hawaiian Climatology", *Pacific Science*, Vol III, 215-225, July 1949, Also at http://eps.berkeley.edu/people/lunaleopold/(024)%20 A%20Review%20of%20Concepts%20in%20Hawaiian %20Climatology.pdf

National Weather Service Forecast Office, *Climate of Hawaii*, January 2007, Also at http://www.prh.noaa.gov/hnl/pages/climate_summar y.php

National Weather Service Forecast Office, *Forecast Area Map* January 2007, Also at www.prh.noaa.gov/hnl/pages/state_zones.php

Office of Hawaiian Affairs *Statewide Public Lands Summary and Maps*,2011, Also at http://www.oha.org/index.php?option=com_content&t ask=view&id=46&Itemid=134

Pidwirny, M. "Climate Classification and Climatic Regions of the World", *Fundamentals of Physical Geography, 2nd Edition*, 2006, Also at http://www.physicalgeography.net/fundamentals/7v.html

University of Hawaii School of Ocean and Earth Science and Technology, *Coastal Geology Group* August 2011, Also at http://www.soest.hawaii.edu/coasts/publications/hawaiiCoastline/oahu.html

Western Regional Climate Center Desert Research Institute, *Climate of Hawaii*, Also at http://www.wrcc.dri.edu/narratives/HAWAII.htm

Chapter Seven: Hawaii's Tropical Environment

Brennan, Barry, *Rodents and Rodent Control in Hawaii,* Research Extension Series, Nov 1980, University of Hawaii, Hawaii Institute of Tropical Agriculture and Human Resources, Also at http://pesticides.hawaii.edu/studypackets/rodents.html

CDC MMWR Weekly, *Maurine Typhus --- Hawaii, 2002*, 52(50);1224-1336, Dec 19, 2003, Also at http://www.cdc.gov/mmwr/preview/mmwrhtml/mm5250a2.htm

EHSO, University of Hawaii, *Mold information for the University of Hawaii,* Aug 2010, Also at http://www.hawaii.edu/ehso/mold.htm

ISSG Global Invasive Species Database, *Monomorium pharaonis (insect)*, Oct 2010, Also at http://www.issg.org/database/species/ecology.asp?si=961&fr=1

ISSG Global Invasive Species Database, Solenopsis papuana (insect), Sep 2009, Also at http://www.issg.org/database/species/ecology.asp?si=955&fr=1&sts=&lang=EN

Kraus, Fred, *Coqui & greenhouse frogs: alien Caribbean frogs in Hawaii*, HEAR project, February 8, 2000, Also at http://www.hear.org/AlienSpeciesInHawaii/species/frogs

Shapiro, Michael, *Day of the Gecko*, Hana Hou: The Magazine of Hawaiian Airlines, Vol 13, No 6, Dec 2010-Jan 2011, Also at http://www.hanahou.com/pages/magazine.asp?Action=DrawArticle&ArticleID=925&MagazineID=59

University of Hawaii Termite Project, *Homeowner's Guide: The secret world of termites*, 2006, Also at http://www2.hawaii.edu/~entomol/guide/secret/index_secret.htm

Yates, Julian, Extension Urban Entomologist, *Scolopendra subspinipes (Leach) – Large Centipede*, December 1992, University of Hawaii, College of Tropical Agriculture and Human Resources, Also at http://www.extento.hawaii.edu/kbase/urban/site/centip.htm

Chapter Eight: Hawaii's Residential Choices

Macomber, Patricia, *Guidelines on Rainwater Catchment Systems for Hawaii*, University of Hawaii at Manoa, College of Tropical Agriculture and Human Resources, 2010, Also at http://www.ctahr.hawaii.edu/oc/freepubs/pdf/RM-12.pdf

Migration Policy Institute Policy Hub, Hawaii: Social and Demographic Characteristics, 2011, Also at http://www.migrationinformation.org/datahub/state.cfm?ID=HI

Neighborhood Commission Office, Neighborhood descriptions, Honolulu City, Sept 2011, Also at http://www1.honolulu.gov/nco/maps/nbbound.htm

Chapter Nine: Hawaii's Complex Property Zoning

Land Use Commission, Department of Business, Economic Development & Tourism, *State Land Use Law (Chapter 205, Hawaii Revised Statutes),* Also at http://luc.state.hi.us/about.htm

Garovoy, Jocelyn, *"Ua koe ke kuleana o na kanaka" (reserving the rights of native tenants): Integrating Kuleana Rights and Land Trust Priorities in Hawaii*, Harvard Environmental Law Review, Vol 29/2005/No 2, p523

Hawaii Revised Statutes, Chapter 7 Miscellaneous Rights of the People, Section 7-1, Also at http://www.capitol.hawaii.gov/hrs2009/Vol01_Ch0001-0042F/HRS0007/HRS_0007-0001.htm

Hawaii Revised Statutes, Chapter 205 State Land Use Commission, Also at
http://luc.state.hi.us/docs/hrs_chapter205_web.pdf

Hawaii Rural Development Council, *Introduction to Hawaii's Land Classification and Management System: A Manual for Residents*, Feb 2008, Also at http://www.hawaiirdc.org/docs/HRDCLandUseManual.pdf

Chapter Ten: Hawaii's Unique Culture

Keller, Larry, *Prejudice in Paradise: Hawaii has a racism problem*, Southern Poverty Law Center Intelligence Report, Fall 2009, Issue Number 135

NPR, *Hawaii is Diverse, But far from a racial paradise*, Nov 15, 2009, Also at http://www.npr.org/templates/story/story.php?storyId=120431126

Index

About the Authors

Tyler and Chris Mercier moved to the island of Hawaii in 2007 and currently live near the beach in Kailua-Kona. They traded in their fast-paced life in Silicon Valley for a laid-back, tropical life in Hawaii. They write blogs, articles, and websites about living and having fun in Hawaii.

The Mercier's blog is hiloliving.blogspot.com. Their websites are hiloliving.com and funhawaiitravel.com and calculatedliving.com.

They value your comments and are happy to answer any questions. Email them at calculatedliving@gmail.com

Find more online resources about building and buying a home in Hawaii at www.YourIdealHawaiiHome.com

Made in the USA
San Bernardino, CA
28 December 2015